"Every new parent wonders, 'What does my baby
need?' *Checklist for Your New Baby* tells you what to
do, what to buy, when to economize and when to get
the very best."

—Dr. Maria I. New
   Chairman, Department of Pediatrics
   The New York Hospital–Cornell Medical Center

"This well-researched marketing list will help you navigate the bewildering maze of baby products and make
safe, economical choices. If you're expecting a baby,
you need *Checklist for Your New Baby*."

—Dr. Adele M. Checchi
   Assistant Professor of Pediatrics
   The New York Hospital–Cornell Medical Center

CHECKLIST FOR YOUR NEW BABY

□□□□□□□□□□□□

DYLAN LANDIS

A PERIGEE BOOK

Perigee Books
are published by
The Putnam Publishing Group
200 Madison Avenue
New York, NY 10016

Library of Congress Cataloging-in-Publication Data

Landis, Dylan, date.
Checklist for your new baby / by Dylan Landis.
p.   cm.
ISBN 0-399-51657-3 (pbk: alk. paper)
1. Infants—Care—United States.   2. Infants' supplies—United
States.   3. Nurseries—United States—Equipment and
supplies.
I. Title.
HQ774.L32   1991
305.23'2—dc20   90-25434 CIP

Printed in the United States of America
2   3   4   5   6   7   8   9   10

This book is printed on acid-free paper.
∞

TO ARI AND DEAN

ACKNOWLEDGMENTS

I talked to dozens of mothers before writing this book, but five good friends were particularly generous with their time and expertise: Barbara Brotman, Catherine Collins, Mare Earley, Lisa Skolnik, and my cousin Stacey Gibbs, a pediatric nurse. They have twelve children among them, and they all knew exactly what my newborn needed, even on the rare occasions when they disagreed.

Many thanks to Dr. Don Brown, Ari's pediatrician in Chicago; Ellen McManus, lactation specialist for the Association for Women's Health Care, Chicago ; Anne Pavlich and Pat Fairall at the U.S. Consumer Products Safety Commission; Janet Schneider at William Carter Company; and two very helpful retailers: Ira Hymen, owner of Bellini in Chicago, and John McKierman, owner of Miller's in Mamaroneck, N.Y.

I would also like to thank Judy Linden at G.P. Putnam's Sons for her vision and encouragement; Dominick Abel, my agent, for his good counsel; Erica Landis and Dean Banquet for great editing on the home front; and Bern Landis for his invaluable support.

Finally, without Ari's baby-sitters, Mary Cruz Gutierrez and Fabiola Zarate, this book could not have been written.

CONTENTS

HOW TO USE THIS BOOK

Four months after I learned I was carrying Ari, my obstetrician, Phyllis Marx, found a fibroid tumor in my uterus. It was the size of a small lime—nothing dire, Dr. Marx said, as long as I went directly to bed and stayed there for the next five months. You can walk to the kitchen or the bathroom, she conceded, but don't even *think* about painting the nursery.

When I called my editor at the *Chicago Tribune* to tell her I wouldn't be back, I was crying, and not because of the tumor, either. I loved my job as a design writer; it took me all the way to Milan once a year, and gave me entrée to some of the most beautifully decorated houses in the world. Lounging around for five months sounded like punishment, not a vacation.

On top of that, my womb was sending out signals as strong and direct as my obstetrician's orders. *Buy me Laura Ashley wallpaper borders for my nursery,* it demanded. *Buy me a white crib, a dove-gray stroller, a playpen, and a swing. Buy me rompers, creepers, sleepers, buntings.* Like the bowerbird, I was becoming a compulsive nest builder.

"Your baby can sleep in a bread box; he won't know the difference," Dr. Marx insisted.

But the mommy hormones were raging. My reporter's

instincts were high, too. So after seven years of writing for newspapers and magazines, I simply set up my own office—in bed. My goal: to be perfectly prepared for this baby, down to the last diaper pin. I might not be allowed to shop, but I could certainly draw up the world's greatest shopping list and hand it to my husband, a *Tribune* reporter who knew even less about babies than I.

I started with books, taking detailed notes, looking for lists I might use myself. The books taught me a lot about product safety, but I still wasn't sure what my baby did (and didn't) need. So I asked several girlfriends with babies of their own to write lists of everything I should buy. I laid their lists out side by side, and tried to figure out why they differed. I called everyone I knew with a baby—an informal survey that took in Chicago, Washington, and New York—and had long, animated talks about such subjects as why babies need undershirts, whether the undershirts should snap closed at the sides or at the crotch, and why some parents loved battery-operated swings while others preferred the windup kind.

New mothers love to talk about babies. My files grew fat. Somewhere around the eighth month, Dr. Marx freed me to take short walks—two or three blocks, she said, and slowly.

Instead I took taxis to the best juvenile stores and lumbered down the aisles, eight months and forty pounds pregnant, quizzing store owners about strollers and snowsuits while calculating distances in the back of my mind: was it half a block from changing tables to cribs, or had I overstepped the three-block limit?

By the time Ari was born, friends of friends began calling, asking for The List. Even our pediatrician learned of it from another patient and wanted a copy. And over the course of a year, with the help of Ari—who gave me full-time, firsthand experience—and a lot of knowledgeable parents, The List grew into a book.

You're reading it now—a checklist for your new baby.

In this book, I've tried to do what most parents can't find the time to do—navigate through a dizzying array of odd-looking products you never even thought about buying before, and then make the simplest, safest, most economical choices.

Your mother didn't have to make those choices; she had only one kind of diaper—cloth—and one way to close it: pins. You can choose between regular disposables, biodegradable ones, and cloth; prefolded or fitted cloth diapers; waterproof diaper covers, water-resistant diaper covers, and plastic pants; diaper clips versus pins; thin diaper wipes in cannisters versus thick ones in boxes.

Finished with diapers? How do you choose between a carriage and a stroller, a battery-operated swing and the windup model, a digital thermometer or the glass one you grew up with?

This is one mother's well-researched way out of the baby-products maze. I've made a lot of judgment calls, based on my own experience and that of other moms. Some parents are going to disagree with certain points. But how you outfit your baby's nursery is a series of highly personal decisions—and all I can promise you is that my way works.

Work from These Shopping Lists

Every major type of product—clothing, car seats, diapers, furniture—has its own chapter, and the key to every chapter, right at the beginning, is its checklist. The checklists are super-specific marketing lists you can literally take to the store. They tell you precisely what products you need, how many to buy, and what key features to look for. *Any item marked with an asterisk* is optional.*

The checklists are brief, to help you speed through your shopping. If an item raises questions, keep reading—you'll probably find a detailed explanation in the notes that follow each checklist.

In those notes I'll tell you how to save money by improvising certain products instead of buying them, how to tell if a secondhand item is safe, and how to pick out the best product in a jungle of look-alikes. I even tell you which essential-looking items—like baby powder and baby bathtubs—your newborn can do very nicely without.

You'll rarely see references to a specific brand or model number, because products frequently change. Instead, I've reported on the best (and worst) features to watch for when you shop.

Finally, there's a timetable in the appendix, a list of everything you may want to accomplish before your baby comes. Even if you can tackle only a few of the items, they'll make your life simpler after the birth.

How to Shop Economically

• For big-ticket items—cribs and strollers, for example—go to big, well-stocked juvenile stores with the best-informed staff (and typically the highest prices). Quiz the owner or manager, try out the products, take your time deciding what you want . . . and then feel free to buy it elsewhere at discount. But I suggest you drop a little money at the store that helped you; in the future, if you need advice, repairs, or refunds, they're more likely to be there for you.

• Make sure you buy only from stores that have a generous refund or exchange policy, and keep everything in its original packaging until you're ready to use it. (Weeks after your baby is born, you may get gifts that duplicate your own purchases.) Instead of trying to keep receipts with each item, which gets messy, make notes on each receipt of what you bought and where, and stick them in a file.

• Comparison-shop. In New York City, five packages of

brand-name diapers (about a month's supply) can cost $55 at a discount drugstore and $70 at a supermarket. Over a year's time, that's a difference of $180.

• Think before you reach for famous brands and special "baby" formulations; sometimes a less-expensive generic or store-brand product has the same ingredients or does the same job. You can save on baby soap, diaper wipes, aspirin substitute, and a host of other products this way.

• If you have to choose between economizing and convenience, opt for convenience—especially when it involves mindless but frequent tasks, like diapering. Take the Vaseline I didn't buy: its money-saving competitor turned out to have a twist-off top. With both hands full of squirming baby, I never managed to screw the top back on; as a result, the petroleum jelly collected dust and stray hairs. Vaseline, and a few savvy store brands, have a flip-top lid that you can replace with one hand. That's the kind of tiny convenience that can outweigh the cost.

Borrow Wisely

Baby products cost a fortune, so when friends offer to lend you something, accept with pleasure. Loans of clothing, linens, a changing table, or late-model car seat can be invaluable. But if the item is a crib or playpen or has any moving parts, especially hinges, and if it wasn't purchased in the last few years, it could be dangerous.

This includes playpens, swings, walkers, toy chests, baby gates, strollers, cribs, and car seats. I've included basic safety information for all these products. But if you're borrowing one of these items, I urge you to do a little research on how to gauge the product's safety and how to use it safely, too. Fast and easy sources include:

• The product's manufacturer. Most big companies have toll-free numbers. Ask if the item meets current safety standards (it may have been recalled) and request a copy of the instructions.

• The U.S. Consumer Products Safety Commission, Publication Requests, Washington, D.C., 20207. The CPSC offers two free brochures: "Tips for Your Baby's Safety" and "The Safe Nursery, a Buyer's Guide." Both contain tips for sizing up the safety of a secondhand item.

• The Danny Foundation, 3160F Danville Blvd., P.O. Box 680, Alamo, CA, 94507. Call (800) 83-DANNY to request a copy of the brochure "Is Your Crib Safe?" A small donation to cover postage is appreciated.

• Two excellent books on product safety are: *Guide to Baby Products,* a Consumer Reports book by Sandy Jones and Werner Freitag, and *The Childwise Catalog* by Jack Gillis and Mary Ellen R. Fise.

What If You Can't Shop before Your Baby's Born?

Some parents are following Jewish tradition, which forbids buying clothes and presents for a new baby until after he is born. Others don't know their baby's gender, which confuses the pink-or-blue question. Finally, some mothers are completely bed bound, which makes shopping impossible.

One way to respect Jewish tradition and still be prepared for your baby is to shop without spending money: choose what you want, from crib to clothing, and ask the store to hold the items until your baby is born. Ideally, you can phone from the hospital, pay with a credit card number, and arrange for quick delivery.

To get around the pink-or-blue issue, you can either (a) buy everything in white, a terrific color for babies, and several primary colors, or (b) pick out your whole layette or baby wardrobe at once, and have the store deliver it in the appropriate pastel once you've telephoned from the hospital. (Don't waffle by purchasing everything in yellow and mint unless you're wild about those colors.)

If you're bed bound, be reassured that anyone can shop from these lists without making mistakes. But a pregnant mom needn't be laid up to share the shopping responsibility. Putting together your baby's nursery is a great start for a nonsexist division of labor—and an expectant parent who spends his or her Saturday picking out a crib is bound to come home with an even deeper feeling of involvement.

I wish you happy shopping, a joyous delivery, and a baby who sleeps through the night.

READER'S NOTE

On the checklists that follow, all items marked with an asterisk (*) are optional.

Also, you'll probably notice that every baby in this book is referred to as "he"—but that's only because my own baby is a boy.

1

BABY CLOTHES

A pregnant woman's first craving isn't for pickles; it's for diminutive dresses and tiny Cat-in-the-Hat stretch suits. Try not to buy them until after the baby shower: at least half your friends will bring gifts of clothing. (The other half will bring stuffed animals.)

Until you try everything on your baby, don't cut the tags off his new clothes—not even when the label says to launder before wearing. You need those tags to make returns. Some things will be out of season by the time they fit; or you might decide to return anything decorated with bunnies.

Finally, don't put too much stock in clothing names. What one company considers undershirts, another may call rompers, creepers, or bodysuits. (Often they make up their own names, like Jamakins and Mufflings.) I've tried to use names as generally as possible.

Here are summer and winter clothing lists, followed by notes on sizes and styles.

Summer Baby Checklist

☐ **6 short-sleeved undershirts with snaps at crotch, size 6 months**

A neat summer outfit all by itself. Shoulders that overlap or snap make dressing easier. In white and pastels, this garment is called an undershirt; in bright colors, stripes, and prints, it's sometimes called a romper.

Spring babies: add 2 long-sleeved, snap-crotch undershirts, size 6 months, to this checklist.

☐ **4 drawstring nightgowns (one size only)**

Nightgowns tie closed at the bottom with a drawstring, and are the easiest garments to open for middle-of-the-night diaper changes. If you prefer, buy lightweight sleepers—loose-fitting outfits with long legs and, as a rule, feet—or stretch suits, in size 6 months.

☐ **2 summer outfits, size 6 months**

Any one-piece outfit with snaps at the crotch.

☐ **2 lightweight cotton sweaters, size 6 months**

Cardigans are easier than pullovers.

☐ **6 pairs of socks, newborn size**

☐ **2 cotton sun hats with brim, newborn size**

☐ **6 cloth bibs**

Look for big terry-cloth bibs that sop up drool and protect clothes.

☐ **3 receiving blankets**

These are 28-inch squares of flannel or cotton knit, used for swaddling the baby. They also make perfect crib or carriage blankets.

Winter Baby Checklist

☐ **4 long-sleeved undershirts with side snaps, size 6 months**

Layer an undershirt under warmer outfits. Because it doesn't reach down to the crotch, you won't have to change it every time your baby's diaper leaks.

Fall babies: Add two short-sleeved, snap-crotch undershirts, size 6 months, to this checklist.

☐ **4 nightgowns (one size only)**

These are the easiest garments to open for middle-of-the-night diaper changes. For moderate warmth, buy drawstring nightgowns, which tie closed at the bottom. For greater warmth, look for fuzzy gowns (sometimes called blanket sleepers) that resemble a sleeping bag with sleeves, and open with a zipper down the front.

☐ **4 sleepers or stretch suits, size 6 months**

Sleepers are loose-fitting outfits with long legs and, as a rule, feet. Stretch suits fit more snugly. Layer them under nightgowns in extreme cold.

☐ **4 long-sleeved jumpsuits or coveralls, size 6 months**

Make sure the legs snap open from crotch to ankle.

☐ **6 pairs of thick socks, newborn size**

☐ **2 warm hats, newborn size**

Hats should cover the ears and not feel scratchy. Babies lose most of their body heat through their heads, so look for something thick and warm.

☐ **1 baby-sized scarf**

Wrap it around his mouth and neck in cold weather.

☐ **1 snowsuit with feet, or a bunting**

For a September baby, buy a snowsuit, size 12 months. He'll swim in it now, but it will still fit him next March. A hood is a nice plus—pull it up over a regular hat if it's really frigid out.

For a December baby, buy a snowsuit, size 6 months.

For a March baby, buy a bunting (one size only, for new-borns). Make sure it has openings to accommodate the car-seat straps. Avoid buntings or "cocoons" that don't cover shoulders and arms.

□ **6 cloth bibs**

Look for big terry-cloth bibs that sop up drool and protect clothes.

□ **3 receiving blankets**

These are 28-inch squares of flannel or cotton knit, used for swaddling the baby. They also make perfect crib or carriage blankets.

NOTES

How Sizes Work

Baby wear always runs small. First-time moms enjoy the tiny newborn or layette sizes that fit neatly right away (and last about a week). But experienced moms start with 6-month sizes, and that's what you'll find on this checklist.

Here's an approximate rule of thumb for sizes. For babies less than one year old, multiply age (in months) by two, and round up to nearest size. Baby sizes start at 3, 6, 9, and 12 months, skip to 18 months, and skip again to 24 months. If results are baggy, just call it room for growth.

BABY'S AGE	SIZE RANGE
newborn	3 to 6 months
3 months	6 to 9 months
6 months	12 to 18 months
9 months	18 to 24 months

How Much Clothing Should You Buy?

My checklists are conservative. They'll give you a dozen outfits for your newborn, including sleepwear. In contrast, the Baby Dior layette list would have you buy eighteen to twenty-six outfits.

Here's my reasoning: you'll have to run the washing machine about every other day because of spit-up stains and diaper leaks. So why buy enough clothing to last a week? Three days' worth is ample, and you can count on four clothing changes a day.

This checklist assumes you share living quarters with a washing machine. If the nearest laundromat is two blocks away, buy 50 percent more of everything, except the snowsuit, and aim for two washes a week.

Look for Soft, Easy-Care Clothing

The best baby clothes have snaps instead of buttons. Snaps are faster, and buttons fall off. (Sweaters are an exception, but make sure the buttons are sewn on tightly, so they don't get swallowed by teething babies.)

In addition, the best baby clothes . . .

- Fasten down the front, not the back. You don't want to flop the baby over while getting him dressed; he'll cry.
- Snap open at the crotch, so you're not pulling them off for diaper changes. If the legs are long, they snap all the way down to the feet, again for easy access.
- Have zippers that won't jab your baby in the neck. A button closure at the top of the zipper prevents this.

In addition, feel around for anything that might bother your baby. Are there any rough edges on labels, seams, or the backs of appliqués? Can you snip off any pom-poms, bells, or ornamental buttons that might come loose and present a choking hazard?

Why All Those Undershirts?

Babies loll about in cotton undershirts much of the time, so you'll find them at the top of the checklists. The neatest ones are long and snap closed at the crotch; depending on the brand, they're called one-piece undershirts, Onesies, rompers, bodysuits, or creepers. They make terrific summer outfits.

In winter, however, buy the side-snap undershirts with long sleeves. They snap open and closed in the front, just off-center, which is easier than struggling with a pullover. (Newborns don't like pullovers; they hate having their faces trapped in the fabric. Remember that when you're tempted by turtlenecks.) You'll be layering these undershirts under warmer clothes, and because they come only to the belly, you may not have to change them when the diaper leaks.

A Note on Receiving Blankets

These soft, square blankets literally receive your baby at birth: your obstetrician will securely swaddle him in one like a gift-wrapped package. (This wrapping not only keeps him warm, it prevents his limbs from flailing in empty space, a sensation that newborns appear to hate.) A receiving blanket is marginally heavier than a flannel sheet, and works nicely as a regular blanket in the stroller and crib, not just for swaddling.

Make sure that you learn how to fold the blanket origami-style for swaddling before you leave the hospital. I stopped swaddling Ari after ten days, but my neighbor swaddled her infant son for nearly five months. Listen to your baby. If he loves being swaddled night and day (you'll know; he'll cry when the wrapping works loose and fall silent when you make it snug), you may want to buy a few more blankets.

Look For Flame-Resistant Sleepwear

New parents are increasingly putting their babies to bed in pure-cotton clothes. But federal law says that anything sold as children's sleepwear must stop burning when you remove it from a fire. Most flame-resistant sleepwear is 100 percent polyester; some is chemically treated cotton. If the thought of synthetics and chemicals repels you, remember that pure cotton ignites in a flash.

Flame-retardant sleepwear is what the baby wears at night, while *you're* sleeping. It doesn't matter what he wears during daytime naps, so long as you're awake.

If the packaging or labels say "sleepwear," "pajamas," or "nightgown," the fabric is flame resistant.

A word about nightgowns, sleepers, and stretch suits: nightgowns are best for nighttime wear—they're soft, loose fitting, warm, and a cinch to open for diaper changes. Sleepers (loose-fitting one-piece pajamas) and stretchies (snug-fitting one-piece pajamas) have to be unsnapped from ankle to waist for every diaper change. You don't need this hassle at 3 A.M. I prefer sleepers to stretchies because they're loose fitting—stretchies need replacing when they get snug in the body or the feet.

Incidentally, nightgowns, sleepers, and stretch suits make great round-the-clock clothing. No one has ever pointed at an infant and said, "What's he doing in his pajamas at noon?"

Socks Are Best for Tiny Feet

They stay on (usually), and you can tell when they get tight. Knitted booties fall right off the feet, and shoes grow tight without your noticing. (Your baby won't complain; the flexible bones in his feet are easily compressed.) Woolly socks even make the best mittens in winter because of their staying power.

You can layer socks for extra winter warmth—and here's what to do with all those loose-fitting booties you've received as gifts: slip them over the woolly socks when you take your baby outside. Given warm socks in winter, your baby won't need shoes until he starts to walk.

Winter Babies: Bunting or Snowsuit?

A bunting is a thick sleeping bag with sleeves—deliciously warm and quickly outgrown. It fits only newborns, so it only makes sense to buy a bunting if your baby is born near the end of winter. (Otherwise, when he outgrows it, you'll have to buy a snowsuit, too.) Be sure the bunting has an opening for the car seat straps, or zips into a snowsuit shape to accommodate the straps.

Buy a bunting or snowsuit you can easily wipe clean and wash.

And now a word from your newborn baby: he keeps his arms and legs curled up close to his body, and hates having them outstretched. Let him keep his arms at his sides, and zip up the snowsuit with empty sleeves.

A good rule of thumb is to dress your baby exactly as you're dressed—if you're comfortable in a T-shirt, he needs just a T-shirt, too. (Babies overheat quickly, which is why you should never bundle up a feverish infant.) One exception: he needs a hat to protect him from the sun, and to keep him from losing heat when it's chilly. Your baby's hands and feet will normally be cool, even when he feels toasty inside.

2

LINENS FOR BED AND BATH

For new parents, an infant's crib is emotionally loaded. Its primary purpose is to keep the baby safe, but parents tend to see it as a soft, secure extension of the womb. We bought simple cotton bedding from a discount store, with a dust ruffle to soften the lines of Ari's crib. But many parents dream of a lavish and beribboned crib. If this is your place to splurge, so be it.

Shop for crib sheets whenever you like, but don't buy linens for your newborn's first little bed—a bassinet, cradle, or portable crib—until you've actually bought that piece of furniture. (You might end up improvising with something less expensive—see Nursery Furnishings, chapter 6.)

First–Baby-Bed Checklist

☐ **2 fitted sheets, sized for bassinet, cradle, or portable crib**

For between-laundry emergencies, slip the mattress into a pillowcase.

☐ ***1 set of fabric bumpers for cradle or portable crib**

Only cradles and portable cribs need bumpers; bassinets are already padded on the sides. Bring mattress measurements when you shop.

Crib and Bath Checklist

☐ **3 fitted sheets made of cotton knit**

Cotton knit is stretchier than plain cotton and easier to put on the mattress.

☐ **2 crib-sized dry-downs**

A dry-down is a thin flannel-and-rubber sandwich—flannel on the outside, rubber in the middle (or flannel on one side, rubber on the other). Placed under a fitted sheet, it protects the mattress from moisture and stains.

☐ **4 lap-sized dry-downs (also called lap pads or puddle pads)**

These rubberized squares can go under your baby's bottom in the stroller or on the changing table.

☐ **1 set of fabric bumpers, sized for crib**

Padded bumpers run around the inside of the crib and keep your baby's head from pressing against the bars.

☐ **Baby blankets or quilts**

For a summer baby, buy one lightweight blanket.

For a winter baby, buy two warm blankets (one might be a down-filled crib quilt). Add receiving blankets as necessary.

☐ ***Dust ruffle**

A luxury—it gives the crib a softer look.

☐ **2 hooded towels**

The hood keeps your newborn's head warm while you dry him off.

☐ **4 baby washcloths**

Washcloths often come with towels in a boxed set. Try to find washcloths that fit your hand like a mitten; they're much easier for scrubbing.

☐ **2 terry-cloth changing-table covers**

Sized to fit the changing-table vinyl pad. (These pads come in more than one size, so buy the changing table first and measure the pad before you shop.)

NOTES

A Word about Sheets

Crib sheets are a tight fit, and the mattress is imprisoned by the crib bars, which makes linen-changing an unwieldy chore. Cotton knit sheets stretch a little, so they're easier to tug over the mattress than plain cotton sheets.

Many layette lists will urge you to buy six sheets, but you don't need that many.

EASY-TO-CHANGE SHEETS WITH VELCRO TIES.

If you dislike wrestling fitted sheets onto the crib mattress, consider a product called E-Z Change-Ups: a top sheet that attaches to the crib rails with Velcro ties. You'll find E-Z Change-Ups in The Right Start Catalog. The idea is terrific; unfortunately, the ties are a little short. To extend them, buy a package of Velcro ribbon from the dime store.

Puddle-Proofing with Dry-downs

These waterproof pads are sized to fit laps, bassinets, and cribs. Don't buy the bassinet size, because those lightweight, plastic-covered mattresses wipe clean with a sponge. Alternatively, two lap pads placed on the little bassinet mattress will give it extra protection against moisture.

Cut down on laundry by placing lap-sized dry-downs, with cotton diapers over them, in the crib under your baby's head and bottom. This also works nicely on the changing table and in the carriage. If neatness counts, consider a product called Crib Bibs—terry-cloth pads that tie to the crib rails, lie under your baby's face, and won't shift around as your baby stirs. You'll find them in stores and in The Right Start Catalog.

Blankets and Bumpers

You already have more blankets than you think. Receiving blankets work nicely in the crib and bassinet; in a pinch, so do fluffy bath towels, or your own bedsheet folded into a square.

Here's what counts most when you're buying blankets: can you throw them in the washer and the dryer? Elaborate handwoven blankets may not live up to the easy-care promises on their labels.

Other than that, woven blankets are better than smooth cotton covers because they're less likely to slide off the baby. But watch out for loose-weave blankets that might catch fingers and toes in the yarn. It sounds like so little to worry about, but for a newborn that trapped toe is traumatic indeed.

FOR A COOL SUMMER CARRIAGE BLANKET . . .

Use a white pillowcase. It keeps the sun off your baby's bare legs without overheating him.

In search of cozy spaces, infants manage to scrunch into the corners of their cribs. Padded bumpers, which run along the sides of the crib, protect their heads. With reservations, I'm recommending fabric-covered bumpers over vinyl ones, largely because they're soft, they last forever—and they're pretty. It really does matter (to parents) that the crib look soft and lovely.

There's a caveat. Fabric bumpers are hard to clean. They can't be tossed in the washer and dryer because they may emerge permanently misshapen. (Don't be seduced by care tags. A Lillian Vernon catalog touts "easy-care machine wash-dry" for its bumpers, but a customer service representative warns on the telephone, "They might get lumpy if you wash them.")

When your fabric bumper gets stained, scrub the dirty spot by hand or have the whole thing dry-cleaned. If the bumper has a removable slipcover, wash that instead. Then you may have the pleasure of pummeling the bumper back inside its mile-long cover.

I longed for vinyl bumpers when Ari had a week-long bout of diarrhea. It stained his white fabric bumpers nearly every day. Vinyl bumpers are ugly, cheap-looking, and given to cracking—but they wipe clean with a sponge.

The Problem with Pillows

Tiny crib pillows, and especially beanbag pillows filled with foam or plastic beads, can suffocate newborns. The Consumer Products Safety Commission considers these pillows very dangerous.

Also missing from this checklist are quilted mattress pads, although they appear on manufacturers' layette lists, and some parents like to use them. Your baby's mattress is already protected from stains and moisture by a dry-down.

MAKING THE CRIB

Arrange dust ruffle on crib frame; put mattress on top.
Cover mattress with crib-sized dry-down.
Cover with fitted sheet.
Attach bumpers, tying strings to corners and sides of crib.

. . . WITH E-Z CHANGE-UPS

Cover mattress with fitted sheet.
Place dry-down on top of sheet.
Cover with E-Z Change-Ups.
Attach bumpers, tying strings to corners and sides of crib.

3

CAR SEATS

All fifty states require car seats; hospitals even insist on them for the ride home. Studies show the biggest car-seat problems come from parents who don't use them properly, strapping the child in too loosely, or forgetting to seat-belt the car seat into the car. Don't rush this purchase—work all the car-seat straps and buckles while you are in the store, and buy a seat you find straightforward and easy to use. Parents who hope to get a car seat as a gift should pick out their favorite brand and model first.

Car-seat checklist

☐ **Infant car seat**

Car owners may prefer a two-part car seat, consisting of a base that stays seatbelted in the car and a seat that snaps easily in and out. If you don't own a car, buy a standard one-piece car seat. A vinyl lining is easier to clean; if you prefer fabric, make sure it's very easy to remove or wash or you'll need to buy a separate fabric liner, too.

☐ **Fabric car-seat liner**

Vinyl-lined car seats are searing hot in summer, cold in winter—they *must* be covered with a separate fabric liner.

I'd also consider this separate liner even for a cloth-covered car seat; it's easy to whip off and throw in the wash.

☐ ***Head-support pillow**

This pillow nestles your baby's head in a kind of padded halo, and keeps it from lolling to one side. You can also use this in the stroller and swing.

NOTES

Quick-and-Easy Car-seat Explanation

There are two kinds of car seats: *infant car seats,* which are molded, padded plastic tubs in which your baby reclines, and *convertible car seats,* which are bigger, and adapt to infants or toddlers. The convertible car seat sounds like a money saver, since you'll need it anyway when your baby's about six months old.

Buy the infant car seat. It will fit your newborn better. It reclines more, increasing the chances of a nap. It has a handle for easy carrying. And it lifts out of the car, so you can carry your sleeping baby into the house. A convertible car seat weighs a ton; you have to leave it in the car.

If you own a car, buy a two-part infant car seat; leave the base permanently strapped in the car and use the snap-out seat to carry your baby indoors. It will double as an infant seat—a little lounge chair in which your infant will spend much of his time.

> If your baby's head flops forward in his infant seat, tip the seat back a little by wedging a blanket under its base. Use the blanket to cover the buckle and shield when your car is parked in the sun; they can burn your baby if allowed to get hot.

The safest place for the car seat is in the center of your backseat, in case your car is struck from the side. Your baby must face backwards, so the impact is distributed along his back, the strongest part of his body.

There's one exception to this backseat rule. If you're driving alone and keep twisting around to see your baby, put him in the front passenger seat, again facing the rear. He's not quite as safe there, but on the other hand, you're far less likely to have an accident when your eyes are on the road.

> If your seat belt is continuous with the shoulder belt (in other words, it's all one long belt), or if the buckle slides freely along the belt, use the locking clip that comes with your car seat. Without it, the car seat can fly out of position in a crash.

How to Buy a Convertible Car Seat

If a relative is clamoring to get you one early, here are the basic guidelines.

Buy the best seat that you're likely to use correctly all the time.

Convertible car seats have two kinds of restraint systems. The *five-point harness* is the safest—it's the same kind of harness used by race-car drivers. Five straps meet in a buckle at your baby's abdomen, crossing his shoulders, his thighs, and his crotch. Try adjusting and buckling everything several times in the store, changing the strap lengths as if to accommodate a fat snowsuit, then a lightweight outfit. Some parents find this so bothersome that they don't adjust the straps properly. If you're not the obsessively careful type, this isn't the car seat for you.

The *three-point retractable harness with shield* is easier to use—it has only one buckle, and nothing to adjust. You pull the harness over the child, and snap it into a buckle between his legs. Attached to the harness is a fat, flat piece of plastic— that's the shield, which covers the abdomen and spreads out the force of impact in a crash. The harness is retractable, so it gives when your child moves forward, but gets snug again when he sits back.

A word about this car seat: it puts a slender stalk of plastic between the child's legs. According to Consumer Reports, it's possible (but not proven) that the stalk could injure the baby if he's slammed into it during a crash. But it's better to use this hassle-free model correctly than a five-point harness incorrectly.

When you're buying a three-point harness car seat, *make sure the straps are retractable.* Otherwise they lock into place, and if your child wants to lean forward, he'll turn blue in the face trying to budge them. If you're buying a five-point harness car seat, however, you probably won't find one with retractable straps—but in our experience, these straps aren't particularly bothersome.

A Word about Borrowing Car Seats

Make sure any car seat you borrow was made after January 1, 1981—that tells you it has passed a tough new safety standard. You'll find the date on a label somewhere on the car seat.

Also check that the car seat is not one of the 30-plus models that have been recalled since 1981. You can obtain a list of recalls by writing the Center for Auto Safety, 2001 S Street, NW, Suite 410, Washington, D.C., 20009.

All car seats come with printed instructions. If you borrow one that doesn't, call or write the manufacturer for a copy. These are the major companies' numbers:

Century	(800) 837-4044
Evenflo	(800) 356-2229
Fisher-Price	(800) 334-5439
Gerry	(800) 525-2472
Graco	(800) 345-4109

Finally, if the car seat was made before February 26, 1985, you may not be able to use it on an airplane. All car seats made after that date, however, are airline approved.

4
TOILETRIES

You wouldn't think one little baby requires so much space in the medicine cabinet, but many of these products are indispensable: thermometers, aspirin substitute, safety scissors for trimming sharp fingernails. They're all very simple to buy.

In fact, the only surprises here are the products you *don't* need—including some you thought no baby could do without, and some that may even be harmful. These are covered after the checklist.

Toiletries Checklist

☐ **2 bottles acetaminophen (aspirin substitute) for infants**

Common brands: Tylenol, Tempra, Panadol. The infant formula comes with a little eyedropper for squeezing medicine into your baby's mouth. Don't refill the bottles with children's formula; the dosages are different.

☐ **1 digital baby (rectal) thermometer**

This plastic thermometer is faster, safer, and easier to read than the glass thermometers you grew up with.

☐ **1 container liquid baby soap**

It's tear free, and it works perfectly on hair, too—no need to buy shampoo.

☐ **1 jar petroleum jelly**

Use on dry bottom to prevent diaper rash. A pull-off lid is easier to manage than a screw-top jar when you're holding a squirming baby and have only one hand free.

☐ **1 tube of diaper-rash cream with zinc oxide**

Heals diaper rash. The ingredient zinc oxide is favored by pediatricians. Common brand: Desitin.

☐ **1 pair baby or safety scissors**

Manicure sized, with rounded ends, for trimming nails and hair. (Try it while he sleeps.) Babies do scratch their faces by accident, but don't solve the problem with protective hand mitts—that muffles their exploration of your skin, the blankets, and the rest of their tiny worlds. Instead, keep their nails short.

☐ ***1 pair of miniature nail clippers**

Some parents find these easier to use than scissors, but try the scissors first; you'll need them anyway for unruly locks of hair.

☐ **2 silicone orthodontic pacifiers**

An orthodontic pacifier has a ball-shaped tip and is sized specifically for newborns. Silicone is a clear, strong plastic; vinyl is also good. Common brands: Evenflo, Gerber, Kip. Avoid rubber or latex if you can; they rot after a couple of months.

☐ **3 large boxes of diaper wipes**

Unscented and alcohol free, so they won't aggravate any allergies or dry out your baby's skin.

☐ ***1 diaper-wipe warmer**

Diaper wipes feel icy in winter. The warmer, purely a luxury, wraps around the container like a heating pad. If wipes dry out, pour a little water on them.

☐ **1 hot-water bottle with cloth cover**

Filled with warm, not hot, water, this can bring middle-of-the-night relief for ear infections, stomach aches, and even chilly crib sheets in winter.

☐ ***1 humidifier**

If your throat hurts from breathing dry, heated winter air all night, your baby's throat may hurt, too. A humidifier can help, but because of possible health hazards it should be filled with demineralized or distilled water, and scrubbed out daily. (Don't buy a vaporizer, which emits hot steam and can be dangerous in a nursery.)

☐ **1 firm-bristled hairbrush**

A little plastic one, for gentle scalp scrubbing, is much better than a sterling-silver brush with his monogram. It stimulates the scalp, preventing (hopefully) a form of infant dandruff called cradle cap. But don't buy this yet—the hospital may send you home with one.

☐ **Bathing sponge**

A two-foot-long sponge with a baby-shaped indentation in the middle. Also called a bath aid.

☐ **1 container of baby-formulated sunscreen, s.p.f. 30**

Dr. Spock puts it this way: "The best thing for sunburn is not to get it." Infants burn faster than grown-ups, so apply sunscreen liberally. Try to make it a massage, not a battle. Keep the cream off tiny hands: it can nauseate an infant who sucks on his fingers, and sting his eyes if he rubs them.

☐ ***Olive, almond, or coconut oil**

For baby massage. (If you don't like the oiliness, use baby lotion instead.) Babies thrive on physical affection, and massage is a deeply relaxing and intimate form of touch. A good book on this is *Loving Hands,* by Frederick Leboyer.

☐ **1 bottle teething topical painkiller**

Apply with a clean finger when teething starts (as early as 3 months).

☐ **Ice pack**

To bring down the swelling of a nasty bump. Don't bother for minor bumps; it isn't worth the trauma. As a backup (if you run out of ice), keep two bags of frozen peas or corn kernels in the freezer. When one loses its "cool," switch to the other.

☐ **Nasal syringe**

To unclog stuffed-up noses. The common two-piece syringe with a removable plastic tip is useless; fortunately some hospitals provide a one-piece rubber syringe.

☐ **2 bottles of syrup of ipecac**

Essential in case of poisoning. Keep one bottle at frequently visited grandparents' house. (Always call your state's poison control center before giving syrup of ipecac to a baby.)

NOTES

Here's What You Don't Need

Baby powder. Believe it or not, you don't need this item. Some brands contain talc, and airborne talc particles can lodge in a baby's lungs. A few older babies have died from mistaking an open powder container for their milk bottle and giving it a good suck.

If you must, tap some cornstarch into your palm (don't send a cloud of it into the air)—but some pediatricians say powder just dries out the skin.

Moisturizer. This isn't harmful, but it also isn't necessary. Infants have tiny pores, and moisturizers may clog up the works. Your newborn's skin may look parched, but if you leave it alone, the flaking stops.

Cotton swabs. Potentially dangerous when poked into ears and noses, especially if the baby moves suddenly. Only your pediatrician should forage in these tiny passages.

Scented baby products. If they give your child a headache, he can't let you know.

Thermometer substitutes. Heat-sensitive pacifiers, or strips that tape to the baby's forehead, are like an experienced mother's kiss: they will tell you if he has a fever, but not precisely how high.

Baby bathtub. Ari hated his—he slumped to the hard plastic bottom and cried. But he loved his bathing sponge, an 18-inch-long, flat yellow sponge with a baby-shaped indentation in the middle. It held him like a warm, wet mattress and worked fine in the kitchen sink and in our tub. The packaging called it a "bath aid."

> To air-dry the bathing sponge between baths, stuff it in a large mesh laundry bag and hang the bag with S-hooks from the shower rod. Mesh laundry bags (for tossing lingerie into the washing machine) are sold in five-and-dime stores, S-hooks in hardware stores.

If you find that your kitchen sink is always full of dishes at bathtime, or your knees ache from kneeling by the bathtub, then do buy a baby tub. Make sure the bathing sponge fits inside—some of the fancier tubs that prop your baby up are too narrow to hold it. Also make sure your tub has no foam lining glued inside; it's hard to scrub clean if it gets soiled.

Bath thermometer. The best thermometer for water temperature is the sensitive skin on the inside of your wrist.

Buying the Right Pacifier

You'll be given a pacifier in the hospital, but buy a couple of your own, too.

Most pacifiers are made of rubber or latex, but these will

literally rot after your baby sucks on them a couple of months. You can avoid this by buying silicone or vinyl pacifiers—you'll recognize them easily; they're as clear as water.

As for shape, start with an orthodontic pacifier; it has an odd bulge at the tip that babies find appealing. (If yours rejects the orthodontic pacifier, offer him a standard bell-shaped pacifier. The right pacifier is the one your baby likes best.)

Boil the pacifier for five minutes when you first take it out of the package. After that, sterilize it in the dishwasher or wash it with hot soapy water. Remember to carry at least two pacifiers in your diaper bag—one invariably drops to the sidewalk.

Pacifiers are safer than they've ever been, since government safety standards went into effect in 1978. Still, it's good to know the three areas of greatest concern:

- The mouth guard should be nearly two inches wide, so your baby can't suck the entire pacifier into his mouth.
- Two holes in the guard should allow your baby to keep breathing if the guard is pressed against his face.
- You shouldn't be able to pull the nipple and the mouth guard apart.

Never use a string to tie the pacifier to your baby or his crib. If you're tired of groping in the blankets for lost pacifiers, you can clip one to your baby's shirtfront with a Binky pacifier clip. (Obviously, if he's a stomach sleeper, this can be an uncomfortable solution.)

Breathing Easier in the Nursery

No humidifier is perfect. Most humidifiers sold today are ultrasonic; they break up water droplets with sound waves to make mist. They can also break up minerals in the water, spewing out a powdery dust that may be harmful to breathe.

The new "warm-mist" humidifiers appear to be safer: they boil water, cool it off, and emit warm, not hot, mist. The machine isn't hot to the touch, but given the boiling water inside I'd keep it well out of baby's reach—cord, plug, and all. (Common brand: Bionaire.) Also new are "wicking" humidifiers, which use a replaceable paper filter to trap some of the bacteria and dust. (Common brands: Bemis, Sears, Emerson Electric Co.)

If you own an ultrasonic humidifier, here are ways to make it safer:

• Attach a special filter, if your humidifier will accommodate it.

• Try anti-dust tablets or solutions, sold in pharmacies.

• Run humidifier on demineralized or distilled water (it comes by the gallon; have the supermarket deliver it by the case).

• Aim the nozzle away from the crib.

• Don't run the humidifier around the clock.

• Clean the humidifier tank every day, using one ounce of chlorine bleach to one pint of water (a Consumer Reports suggestion). Rinse very well with fresh water.

• Bacteria thrives in moisture, so keep humidity at 30 to 50 percent. To measure, buy a hygrometer for several dollars at a hardware store.

Some humidifiers claim to be designed for the nursery, with built-in night-lights and floating yellow ducks. Floating yellow ducks belong in the bath—why teach your baby that an electrical appliance is a toy?

A Note on Diaper Wipes

Until you've got the hang of changing diapers, buy wipes in boxes, not cannisters. The wipes in boxes are nice and thick (and expensive), and they pull out like Kleenex—a one-handed operation. Wipes in cannisters are thinner and cheaper, and require both hands: one to hold the cannister, the other to yank out a wipe. Your baby will seize the chance to kick his heels into the dirty diaper you've just unwrapped.

WIPE TIPS

When you're out of wipes, squirt baby oil generously onto soft paper towels, toilet paper, or facial tissues.

Pack diaper wipes in a plastic sandwich bag that seals at the top. They travel well, and you won't be paying for expensive travel sizes.

In Case of Emergency

Buy two bottles of *syrup of ipecac*, which can make your baby vomit up whatever substance he gulped down. (The second bottle is for a grandparent's home, which is probably not childproofed.)

If your baby swallows something unknown or dangerous, never give him ipecac until you call your state's poison control hotline for instructions. (The number is in the front pages of your phone book; post it by the telephone and tape it to the ipecac bottles, too.) Two reasons for this caution: caustic substances, like bleach, burn as they go down and will burn doubly if you force them back up. And babies under nine months are rarely given ipecac—nevertheless, this item belongs in your medicine cabinet from the start.

5
STROLLERS

Many parents say the biggest shopping mistake they made was spending money on a pram or carriage—a big, comfortable bed on wheels that's difficult to fold up and then fills the entire car trunk. I loved my pricey carriage—it felt sturdy as a Volvo, had a lift-out bed that I could wrestle, with difficulty, into a sitting position, and was so weatherproof that I walked Ari on the worst days Chicago had to offer. But in six months this beauty landed in permanent storage, having lost out to a less expensive and lighter stroller.

Moral: if you ever plan on schlepping it on the bus or even hoisting it up a flight of stairs, make it a stroller—a lighter, pared-down vehicle—with a reclining seat, so your newborn can sleep. But by all means, if there are no stairs in your life, feel free to borrow—not buy—a pram or carriage for the first few months.

You'll find two kinds of strollers: *umbrella strollers,* which rarely lie back all the way, weigh next to nothing, and can be carried over the wrist (when folded) like a big umbrella; and *standard strollers* that may borrow some features from carriages, like the all-important fully reclining seat. *Buy a standard, reclining stroller* that reclines all the way and folds up easily. Don't try to economize—the cheaper the stroller, the greater its chances of breaking down. Buy your stroller from a store with good sales help, a large selection, and the ability to help you with repairs.

Stroller Checklist

☐ **Stroller**

Key features: fully reclining seat, double wheels, swivel wheels in front, canopy, weight no greater than 16 pounds, easy steering with one hand, and one-hand folding. (If the stroller requires two hands to fold, you may end up laying your baby on the ground.) Given a choice between fabric and vinyl, choose vinyl; it's easier to clean. For twins, buy a stroller with front and back seats, not side-by-side seating.

☐ **Padded fabric liner**

Buy a stroller liner that you can toss in the washer and dryer.

☐ **Under-the-stroller basket**

If this is sold separately, buy it. It carries diapers, small groceries, magazines, whatever you like.

☐ **Plastic rain shield**

Great for rainy days, and transparent, so your baby can see out (and you can see in).

NOTES

Test-driving a Stroller in the Store

Walk it up and down the aisles, checking these points:

• Can both parents push the stroller without kicking their toes into the wheels?
• Can you steer the stroller easily with one hand? (The other may be holding the groceries.)

- Does it turn corners easily?
- Can you work all the parts easily—lock and unlock the seat belt, raise and lower the seat back, open and close the canopy, and fold the stroller up?
- When you push down on one side and, more importantly, on the handle, does the stroller threaten to tip?
- Can you fold the stroller with one hand behind your back?

More Stroller Features

Strollers offer a number of options, some convenient, but none of them essential:

Good balance when folded. It helps if your stroller will stand up by itself when it's folded and locked.

Waterproof "boot." This snaps over the foot of the stroller to cover your baby's legs when it's raining. I think a rain shield does a better job—it covers the entire baby.

Reversible handle. This handle flips from one side of the stroller to the other, so the baby can either face you (when he's lying down) or look out at the world (when he's sitting up). Without a reversible handle, he faces away from you. This is irritating to some mothers, but not a calamity.

The reversible handle makes a stroller heavier, so consider how badly you want a feature that's valuable for only the few months until your baby can sit up. If you'll be carrying the stroller onto public transportation or up a flight of stairs, skip it.

Do check if the handle is shorter in one position than in the other. Also make sure that when you reverse the handle, you can lock the front swivel wheels (now in back) so they stay straight, and unlock the back wheels (now in front) so they swivel.

Seat wide enough to carry an infant car seat. If your baby falls asleep in the car, just place the car seat on the carriage, and wheel the slumbering angel away. Try it out with a car seat in the store.

WHEN STROLLER WHEELS STICK

Almost every stroller gets enough dirt around the wheels so that steering eventually becomes a struggle. You push forward, and the carriage balks or veers right. To make it better (or prevent the problem before it happens), spray between the double wheels with a can of silicone spray from the hardware store.

Do this as often as necessary, but not indoors. Silicone is a lubricant, and I slipped on my wood floors for several days where the stroller had been sprayed. Heaven knows what it does to carpets.

Strollers for Twins

Side-by-side strollers can't be pushed through some doorways—quite a jam to be in when you're trying to buy milk or get into a doctor's office. For that reason alone, I recommend a stroller with a front seat and a back seat. For twin newborns, make sure that both seats recline all the way. If one seat is for a toddler, however, it doesn't need to recline.

The Last Word

By the time your baby reaches toddlerhood, you may decide to fold up your expensive, versatile stroller for the last time and buy a super-lightweight, nonreclining umbrella stroller, like everyone else.

6

NURSERY FURNISHINGS

Your baby doesn't care about the Snoopy wallpaper; he just needs a restful place to sleep. But *you* have to feel terrific in this nursery. You'll be here a lot—nursing, singing, rocking, changing diapers, or simply staring into the crib at this perfect little person.

Decorate the nursery to please yourself. One Chicago interior designer had plaid curtains and hunting prints in her own nursery for a classic, masculine look; it didn't hurt her baby girl one bit. Other decorators who work with children's rooms say parents are tiring of pink and blue, and are using more sophisticated color combinations: lavender, yellow, and green, for example, or pale gray walls with accents of yellow or blue.

These are the basic furnishings you'll need:

Nursery Checklist

☐ ***Bassinet or cradle**

For the first couple of months, most new parents keep the newborn in their own bedroom—but a bassinet (tiny bed) or cradle (tiny bed that rocks) is an expensive, short-lived purchase. I suggest borrowing anything that works as a baby bed, including a pram or carriage. Otherwise, consider buying a portable crib you can travel with later on or give to the baby's grandparents for visits.

☐ **Crib**

All cribs made today must meet federal safety standards. They're hard to assemble; ask the store if you can pay to have this done for you when the crib is delivered. For a second-hand crib, examine it with a tape measure and the guidelines listed after this checklist.

☐ **Crib mattress**

I recommend a high-quality (dense) foam mattress, because it's lighter, and thus easier to change, than an inner-spring mattress. It's also cheaper. But foam breaks down, a victim to time and bouncing. Your next baby will need a new mattress.

☐ **Changing table**

This holds the baby at waist-high level, so you can lay him down and change his diapers without bending and straining your back. I like the basic table with open shelves below, and a safety barrier to keep baby from rolling off. Some bureaus offer fold-out changing platforms on top, but it's hard to open the top drawer with the platform extended, and you must step back from the baby—an unsafe move—to open the others.

☐ **Bureau**

Look for a sturdy bureau with small drawers (easier for a child to keep neat), drawer stops (toddlers like to see how hard they can yank the drawers out), and no brutally sharp corners at toddler's eye level. Don't leap at a bureau that matches the crib; it's expensive, and may not seem so cute when your baby outgrows his crib.

☐ **Rocking chair**

An intimate place for feedings and lullabyes. Make sure that you can outfit it with cushions and that it fits both parents comfortably; a rocking chair that Dad doesn't use is a loss for baby and father both. Your options range from a fully upholstered gliding chair to an unfinished rocker. Pregnant do-it-yourselfers, however, should keep far away from wood-finishing products; the fumes can harm the fetus.

□ **Shelves**

Safer and easier to organize than toy chests, and useful for years. Colorful stacking plastic crates are another alternative.

□ ***Lamp**

Not essential if the nursery has an overhead fixture, but lamps do offer a nice warm light. Safest of all: a wall sconce or two; toddlers can't tip them over. Otherwise, look for table or floor lamps that are sturdy and hard to tip; resist clown-and-balloon sculptures that will soon be outgrown; and avoid halogen if there's any way a toddler might be burned by the bulb.

□ **Night-light**

Buy a new night-light with a UL (Underwriters Laboratories) certification mark; old ones have been known to short-circuit or explode. Look for a simple light that isn't disguised as a toy (why attract a baby to an electrical outlet?) and is easily packed into a suitcase for travel.

□ **Curtains or blinds**

Your newborn can nap in dim light; he doesn't need total darkness. Avoid long curtains—an older baby can pull himself up by the fabric and bring the whole affair down on his head—and long, trailing cords, which can strangle a baby. Roll up the cords and clip them with a clothespin, or wind them around an out-of-reach hook.

□ **Dimmer switch**

By installing a dimmer switch for the overhead light (a fairly simple and inexpensive do-it-yourself project), you can give yourself just enough light for diaper changing without having a 100-watt glare in your eyes at 2 A.M.

NOTES

Bassinets and Their Alternatives

Having just emerged from a small, warm space, your newborn may be uncomfortable in a vast, open desert—like the crib you're about to purchase with so much care. But bassinets are very expensive for something you pack away after three months at best. Here are three good options; pick the one that best fits your circumstances.

1. *My baby needs a second crib at his grandparents' house.* Buy a wooden portable crib (try to get one narrow enough to roll through doorways). Use it in your own bedroom instead of a bassinet, then give it to the lucky grandparents when your baby moves into his nursery.

2. *I need a crib I can travel with, or pull out for visiting babies.* Buy a mesh-sided portable crib and use it now as a bassinet. It has a slender but adequate mattress, packs into a nylon bag for travel, and can double as a playpen later on. As a bassinet it has one disadvantage—you have to stoop over to retrieve your baby. But that's a small inconvenience, considering this little crib will last into toddlerhood.

3. *I really want a newborn-sized bed.* Try to borrow a carriage or pram; it makes a fine bed on wheels. Or borrow a Moses basket, a baby-sized basket with handles. (It's named for the basket that the infant Moses was found in.) Make sure that the handles are firmly attached, that you can't fit two fingers between mattress and basket, and that the basket is well balanced in your hand when you carry it by the handles.

Another option is to buy a swing with a cradle attachment for newborns. At night, you can take it off and use it as a small bassinet for perhaps six weeks.

If you buy a bassinet, buy a sturdy one; babies have been

injured when the bottoms fell out. Push down on the bassinet bottom to see if it gives; push down on the sides to see if it can tip.

Cradles should lock at night so your baby won't roll to one side and get stuck there. (If he's pressed against a heap of covers, he can suffocate.) The rockers of an antique cradle can be held in place with a book on each side. You'll have to buy bumpers for a cradle, whereas a bassinet comes with padded sides.

Buying a New Crib

Some thoughts on testing a crib in the store:

• Work the side rails on different models. Do you prefer stepping on a kick-bar to lower the rail, or working a latch by hand? This is a matter of personal preference, but some women find that holding a baby in the dark while trying to press a bar with one foot can make them lose their balance.

• Does the crib feel sturdy? Compare the store's most expensive cribs with its cheapest and you'll get a sense of what sturdiness is.

• Can you live without ornate styling and lacy canopies? Cribs are expensive; cutting out frills is one way to cut costs.

In a few years your child can graduate from his crib to a twin-sized bed, so don't spend extra money on a crib that converts to a "junior bed." The junior bed is smaller than a twin, requires a specially sized mattress and sheets, and won't even save you from having to purchase a twin bed down the line.

A crib mattress will last longer if you rotate it every few months, turning it onto its other side.

When Is a Used Crib Safe?

Older cribs pose quite a few risks, yet thousands of babies sleep in them. If you can borrow a relatively new crib, terrific—you've just saved several hundred dollars. If you don't know the crib's pedigree, be careful. Here's a list of safety checks from The Danny Foundation, a crib-safety watchdog group.

• Was the crib made before 1978? If in doubt, don't use it. Pre-1978 paint can contain more lead than is currently allowed, and babies do teethe on their cribs.

• Do corner posts extend more than $\frac{1}{16}$ of an inch above the end panels? Nearly fifty babies have died when their clothing caught on the corner posts.

• Slats must be only $2\frac{3}{8}$ inches apart, and none may be loose or missing. Wider space than that poses a strangulation risk if the baby's body or head squeezes through.

• If the crib has been dismantled, put it back together with screws one size larger than the originals to ensure that everything fits together tightly. (If you keep using the old screws, the holes may get wider, and the crib might not hold up as well. Credit for this tip goes to Consumer Reports' book *Guide to Baby Products.*)

• Plastic teething rail should be tightly attached to the side rail, or it can painfully trap an exploring tongue.

• Gap between mattress and crib should not admit two adult fingers. (I'd buy a new mattress for the crib, unless it came with a firm innerspring mattress.)

• Cutout designs in the end panels, even small ones, are dangerous. Babies have died of strangulation when their heads were entrapped.

Buying a Nursery Suite

You may set out to buy a crib and end up staring at sleek Italian room settings, complete with matching bureaus and shelves. The idea behind these expensive suites is that you'll never need to buy new furniture—the changing platform becomes a desk or shelf, while the bureaus keep on providing storage. You'll eventually need a twin bed, however.

If you like the ultra-coordinated look and can afford it, go right ahead. When your child wants a new look, you can change the knobs or paint the trim a different color. Buy white laminate to start with, so it won't clash with any new decorating plans.

Still, I suspect that I could furnish any nursery twice— once for an infant, and again three years later for a little boy—for less than the price of a Eurostyle suite of furniture. First I'd buy a good, simple crib and a basic open-shelved changing table. Then I'd buy unpainted or second-hand wood shelves and bureaus, and finish them myself. When the occupant of the room got bigger and demanded a new decor, I'd help him pick a color, haul the furniture outside, and spray-paint it.

A Bed in the Nursery

If you have the room, a bed or sofa in the nursery is a real comfort—you can lie down to nurse at 3 A.M., and drift off with your baby in your arms. It also gives you extra space for overnight guests.

The Traditional Toy Chest

You can't keep a toy chest in any kind of order—things slip to the bottom and disappear. Then there are the safety hazards. An old chest can be lethal if its lid slams shut on a child's head. A newer chest may be airtight, which is dangerous if a child climbs inside. For the same amount of floor space you can have bookshelves that are useful longer and easier to organize.

Stores that sell toy chests also sell another tempting item—toddler-sized play tables with diminutive chairs, often decoratively painted by artists. Wait: your baby won't need a play table until he's well into toddlerhood. If you do buy one now, make sure it's sturdy and unadorned and won't suffer from crayon marks. Tables decorated with animals or place settings will compete with your child when he sits down to draw, and make it impossible to play spaceship.

A Note on Decorating

Keep the background of the room simple—children like to change their decor as they grow. Instead of a floor-to-ceiling wallpaper design of toy soldiers, for example, you might apply the same pattern in a wallpaper border, first at chair-rail height (36 inches from the floor) and again just under the ceiling. (For high ceilings, drop the border 12 inches.) For greater emphasis, put up the wallpaper inside your baby's closet, and have it professionally bonded to a windowshade. Not only will the pattern pop out with greater clarity, but you can change it later on without re-painting and repapering every inch.

7

NURSING SUPPLIES

Babies don't need any special nursing gear—just milk, which miraculously appears when they cry. But new mothers use all kinds of conveniences: nursing bras, nursing pads, breast pumps, bottles, nipples, formula. Some of these things look like scientific laboratory equipment, and even the simplest things, like baby bottles, will dazzle you with choices. (Do you want the pre-sterilized disposable ones, the conventional plastic ones, or the purple ones shaped like donuts?)

Breast-feeding mothers and bottle-feeding parents have separate lists.

Checklist for Breast-feeding Mothers

☐ **4 plastic bottles, 8-oz. size**

When expressing and freezing breast milk for a baby less than 1 month old, fill these bottles only about halfway. (That's all a newborn can drink.)

☐ **2 silicone or vinyl orthodontic nipples, sized for newborns**

You really need 4, but be sure your baby likes them before you stock up. Some babies prefer a different type of nipple.

☐ **1 package of nipple covers**

These are tall plastic caps that fit over the nipple and the neck of the bottle, keeping the nipple clean and preventing leaks in the diaper bag. They often come three to a package.

☐ **1 bottle brush**

Long and narrow, for scrubbing baby bottles. Look for one with a loop or hole in the handle so you can hang it from a cup hook to dry.

☐ **1 nipple brush**

As narrow as a baby's finger, for scrubbing nipples. Buy one that can be hung up to dry.

☐ **2 cotton nursing brassieres**

Buy them one cup size larger than you need in your last month of pregnancy. Bras unhook from the top or the center; choose whichever seems easier to you.

☐ **2 bra extenders**

Small straps with hooks that can add a size or two to a tight nursing bra. Available in dime stores and some maternity stores, they come in two widths, so bring your bras along when you buy them.

☐ **1 box of disposable nursing pads**

Put the pads in the bra cups to absorb any milk leaks.

☐ **2 nursing shirts**

These shirts have flaps that pull apart or unbutton for discreet breast-feeding in public—a blessing in restaurants or department stores. If you're still buying maternity tops, make sure they can double as nursing shirts.

☐ ***1 nursing nightgown**

A luxury, if you want to breast-feed on a cold winter night without disrobing. Another option: men's flannel pajamas that unbutton down the front.

☐ **Breast pump**

Every nursing mother needs one. I suggest a purse-sized electric or electric/battery pump; they're easiest to use. But if you're on a tight budget, buy a piston- or cylinder-style manual pump.

☐ **4 cans ready-to-use formula, 8-oz. size**

Ask your pediatrician to recommend a brand. Good to have around in case of sudden emergencies (your doctor puts you on medication and warns you not to breast-feed, or a power outage thaws all your frozen breast milk).

Checklist for Bottle-Feeding Mothers

☐ **8 plastic bottles, 8-oz. size**

☐ **2 silicone or vinyl orthodontic nipples, sized for newborns**

You really need eight nipples—but start with two, to see if your baby likes them. Some babies are picky and need to try different kinds of nipples.

☐ **1 package of nipple covers**

These are tall plastic caps that fit standard bottles; they keep the nipple clean and prevent leaks in the diaper bag. They often come three to a package.

☐ **1 bottle brush**

Long and narrow, for scrubbing baby bottles. Look for one with a loop or hole in the handle so you can hang it from a cup hook to dry.

☐ **1 nipple brush**

As narrow as a baby's finger, for scrubbing nipples. Buy one that can be hung up to dry.

☐ ***Electric sterilizer**

Buy this only if you feel strongly about sterilizing bottles before each use.

☐ ***Drying rack for bottles and nipples**

A nice convenience, this wooden rack lines them up neatly for air drying and storage. Sold in The Right Start and other catalogs.

☐ **1 case of concentrate formula**

Ask your pediatrician to suggest either a soy-based or milk-based formula. Beyond that, brand-name formulas are fairly similar; you can pick your own or ask the pediatrician to recommend one.

NOTES

A Word about Bottles

Buy 8-ounce plastic bottles, not the diminutive 4-ounce ones, even though your newborn will drink just a few ounces at a time. The larger size will remain useful as his appetite grows.

Why plastic? It may lack the sparkle of clean glass, but it's easier to carry around, and it won't shatter on the kitchen floor at three o'clock in the morning. Besides, breast-feeding mothers should freeze their milk only in plastic: there's some evidence that the nutrients in frozen breast milk stick to glass; consequently, the thawed milk is a little less nutritious.

Ignore all those bottles adorned with NFL helmets or in colors that prevent you from seeing the liquid inside, and avoid donut-shaped bottles that can't be cleaned thoroughly with a bottle brush.

Some baby bottles are sold with rubber nipples included. I suggest you throw those nipples out and use the silicone nipples on the checklist.

What about Disposable Bottles?

Some mothers swear by them, so it's worth explaining why they're not on my checklist. Disposables are made up of pre-sterilized plastic bags, which hold the milk, and hard plastic tubes, which hold the bags. (Nipples and rings fit over the tubes.) The trick is to fold the edges of the plastic bag over the tube without tearing it. So many parents can't master this that I left disposables off the list.

However, if you've heard rave reviews of disposables from a friend or neighbor, here's a good way to give them a try:

Disposable Bottles Checklist
• Buy the Playtex Baby Nurser Kit, a starter kit of disposable bags, rings, and nipples that you can mail back to Playtex for a refund if you don't like the system.
• Buy only three regular plastic bottles, instead of eight, until you decide which you like better.
• Buy two silicone or vinyl orthodontic nipples for the standard bottles, and two for the disposable bottles. (Disposable bottles typically come with a flat-topped nipple that some babies reject.)

Whatever type of bottles you use, you can store breast milk in the sterile plastic bags designed for disposables. (The bags are sold separately.) My friend Lisa closes the bags with ponytail-sized rubber bands, dates them with little Avery labels from the stationery store, and stands them up in her freezer door.

How to Buy the Right Nipple

A good nipple to start with is a vinyl or silicone orthodontic nipple.

Buy a nipple sized for newborns. Some brands just say "orthodontic," which means they are appropriate for newborns. Some, like Pur, start at size 0–3 months. And others are labeled for different drinks, like Evenflo's choice of milk, water, formula, and juice nipples. (In that case you'd choose milk, for thawed breast milk, or formula.)

As long as your newborn sucks contentedly, the size is

right. If he gags, the opening is too large, and if he struggles and cries, the opening may be clogged up or too small.

If your newborn is picky about nipples, let him try several kinds. Respect his decision; he can't make a bad one. You'll find nipples made from four materials—silicone, vinyl, rubber, and latex—and in two shapes, orthodontic and standard.

Silicone and vinyl nipples are a good first choice: they're clear—a squeaky-clean look that many mothers like—and can survive the dishwasher. Inspect them periodically, because they may tear, although I've never seen it happen. Vinyl is marginally stronger than silicone, but silicone is still quite strong, and it's easier to find in stores.

Rubber and latex nipples are short-lived: they can rot, turn sticky, and generally deteriorate in two to four months. (Your baby's own saliva causes their demise.) If the package isn't clearly labeled, a glance at the nipple will tell you what it's made of—if you can't see through it, it's rubber or latex. (Don't be surprised if it's white or pastel. Some companies seem to be avoiding the traditional amber color.)

When you first feel the stickiness or see a white film inside the nipple, it's time to buy a new one. These nipples can't go into the dishwasher, either.

As for shape, *orthodontic nipples* have a ball-shaped tip that supposedly feels more like a mother's nipple in the newborn's mouth and elicits a more natural type of sucking. Try them first—many babies relish the shape, and some dentists recommend it too.

Standard nipples are bell shaped and are appropriate for babies of any age, including newborns.

Nipples for Disposable Bottles

These used to come only in a flat-topped shape, which some babies didn't like. Finally, manufacturers are offering the same diversity of nipples that you find for standard bottles. Here, too, start with an orthodontic nipple, preferably in silicone or vinyl.

Do You Really Need a Sterilizer?

Bottle-feeding mothers who want to sterilize bottles and nipples before every feeding can buy an electric sterilizer (just plug it in and turn it on) or a sterilizing kettle that boils the bottles on the stove top. The electric sterilizer costs more, but it's worth it for the convenience. However, why bother? Doctors are much more relaxed about sterilizing these days. You can boil the bottles and nipples for five minutes when you first take them out of the package; then wash them in hot soapy water—or, better yet, the dishwasher—after each subsequent use.

If you're breastfeeding and use only occasional bottles, you can pop them in a pot of boiling water and extract them with tongs.

Brassieres for Nursing Mothers

A nursing bra has cups that open, so breast-feeding mothers can offer one breast at a time without disrobing. Start with two bras until you're sure of the style and size. If you wash them daily, you may not need more.

Leave the tags on until after your milk comes in, and only buy from a maternity store that will let you exchange the bras.

How to fit a nursing bra: In your last month of pregnancy, buy a bra that fits comfortably when you hook it, but is one cup size larger than what you need at that time. Examine the bra for these features:

• Easy access to the breast. Some flaps open from the top, others from the center of the bra; buy what seems simplest to use.

- Cotton bra cups.
- Straps made mostly of fabric, not of pure elastic. Elastic stretches and doesn't offer enough support.
- A wide band in back. There's no minimum width, but you want a band broad enough to give you a feeling of support.

Fit underwire bras with special care. If the wire rides up, it can clog your milk ducts.

When your milk first comes in (about forty-eight hours after your baby is born), the bra may feel tight for three or four days. Bra extenders will get you through this period. After that, as the swelling decreases, the fit should be fine. If it isn't, exchange the bras or keep using the extenders.

Bra extenders are indispensable little straps, several inches long, that lengthen a bra by a size or two. Buy them before you need them—a tight bra is very painful to a nursing mother. You can hook two extenders together if necessary.

Milk Stains and Nursing Pads

Most women's breasts leak for a week or two after childbirth, but some women keep leaking as long as they're breast-feeding. An absorbent pad in your nursing bra will prevent the shadowy stains on your shirt.

Start with a box of disposable pads, sold in drugstores and maternity shops. If you're leaking heavily after one box (or two weeks), try washable or homemade pads instead.

Washable pads are round, usually cotton, and about the size of a generous cookie. Buy a pad that puts cotton against your breast, not plastic. You can toss cotton pads in the washing machine, but the dryer will melt any water-resistant backing on the pad.

To prevent a cotton pad from migrating to your armpit, stitch a tuck from the center to the side, creating a shallow cone.

The best *homemade pads* consist of half a thin, sticky-backed sanitary napkin, inserted north-south in the bra; it's super-absorbent and won't slip around.

The Essential Breast Pump

If you're breast-feeding, a pump is crucial. It gives you freedom—you can fill a few bottles for the baby-sitter and take a much-needed night off—and it's a great help if you're trying to clear a clogged milk duct. It lets you return to your job and still give your baby breast milk, or take a few bottles on a shopping trip if you don't care to breast-feed in public. Finally, it lets the father do some of the feeding, an experience he shouldn't miss.

Try to buy your pump from a store that will take it back after you've tried it. Women's breasts are different, so the pump that your best friend loves may be frustrating for you.

Purse-sized electric pumps are the best investment. They're easy to use, which you'll appreciate if you end up pumping milk every day or so. Buy a model that runs on electricity; the battery-only pumps can devour scores of batteries and don't always muster up sufficient power.

However, if you're economizing and you don't plan on expressing milk every day, a *manual pump* is acceptable. Buy a cylinder-style or piston-style pump, which looks like a short bicycle pump and works with the same in-and-out motion. Your arms will ache the first few times, but it gets easier. Avoid squeeze-bulb pumps commonly sold in drugstores, because milk can back up into the bulb and breed bacteria.

Full-sized *electric pumps,* not to be confused with their purse-sized cousins, are big, heavy, and fabulously efficient. They're also so costly that women don't buy them—they rent them by the month. Use this non-portable machine if you express milk several times a day and get nowhere with a purse-sized pump, or if you're separated from your baby and want to keep up your milk supply. This is also an efficient, if expensive, option for the working woman who can keep the pump in a private office.

Buying Formula

A formula-fed baby will drink this concoction until he turns one, so buy it by the case from the cheapest source you can find. Your pediatrician will suggest either a milk-based formula (Enfamil, Similac, and Gerber are common brands) or a soy-based one (such as Isomil). If a brand offers you a choice of iron-added and no-iron formulations, always reach for the can with added iron. Most pediatricians believe that a steady diet of no-iron formula can lead to anemia.

Formula comes three ways: powdered, ready-to-use, and concentrate. Start with concentrate, but try the others later on.

Concentrate formula comes in 13-ounce cans and must be mixed with an equal amount of water. This is easy—you mix it right in your baby's plastic bottles. Once you open the cans, you have to refrigerate the mixture.

Powdered formula comes with its own scoop in 1-pound cans and must be mixed with water. It's the least expensive, and you can make up one bottle at a time, a nice convenience if you don't feel like waiting for a refrigerated bottle to warm up at 4 A.M. But even when it's well shaken, tiny clumps of powder can block the nipple: if your baby starts howling in the middle of a feeding, that's probably why.

Reduce clumping by putting the powder in the bottle first, then adding water, then pinching the nipple tightly shut (or capping the bottle) when you shake the mixture up.

Make sure the powdered formula you buy contains "soy oil" or "soybean oil." It's a key nutritional ingredient, but some powdered formulas don't yet include it.

Ready-to-use formula needs no mixing; you pour it straight from the can into the baby bottle. It comes in 32-ounce and 8-ounce cans, as well as expensive tiny bottles that accept regular rings and nipples.

Breast-feeding mothers should keep a few of the 8-ounce cans in the cupboard for emergencies; car owners can keep the same cans, along with a can-opener and empty baby bottle, in the car.

The little 4-ounce and 6-ounce bottles (depending on the brand) are perfect for plane trips: all you do is unscrew the metal cap, attach a regular nipple, and throw the bottle out when it's empty. Not all supermarkets carry these sizes; you may have to shop around, or ask the market manager to order them.

Save the metal caps from these jars, too—they'll fit on your own baby bottles and prevent leaks in the diaper bag.

Even in unopened cans, formula goes bad if you store it in a hot place, like the car trunk in July. If you see separated layers of liquids when you open the can, return the formula to the store.

Warming a Cold Bottle

Most parents stick the cold bottle in a pot of hot water. If you like conveniences, you can pick up a little appliance called a bottle warmer. Ignore the expensive ones with built-in night-lights, and buy a cheap one in a discount store. Appliance or no, you still have to wait for the milk to warm up, and test it on the inside of your wrist.

A faster alternative, for formula-fed babies only, is the microwave oven, used with great care.

WARMING BOTTLES IN A MICROWAVE, SAFELY

Microwave ovens make parts of the milk in the baby bottle scalding and leave some of it cool, a mixture that can burn your baby's mouth, throat, and esophagus. The only way to use a microwave safely is to *follow this ritual every time:*

☐ Take the lid or nipple off the baby bottle.

☐ Heat the open bottle for short periods (30 to 50 seconds for an 8-ounce bottle, depending on the strength of your microwave).

☐ Shake it violently to blend the hot and cool parts of the liquid.

☐ Test a few drops on the inside of your wrist.

A microwave's heat is far too high for breastmilk and may destroy some of the nutrients.

8

CARRIERS, SWINGS, AND OTHER BABY GEAR

Infant seats, bouncers, walkers, swings . . . why fill your home with these babyish things? Because the bouncer could buy you ten minutes on the phone with your mother. Because the swing could be your ticket to an uninterrupted candle-lit dinner. Never mind the clutter—anything that makes your baby calm and happy will make you grateful beyond words.

Not every infant likes all this equipment, however—some act as if they're imprisoned in the Tilt-A-Whirl and howl until released. Ari screamed so loudly in his Snugli, a front-pouch baby carrier, that I expected the police at my door. (We returned it.) You have two options: let your baby try a friend's gear before you buy anything—or buy the gear in advance, familiarize your baby with it from birth, and return anything he hates. I suggest the latter.

Here's a list of the most useful items.

Gear Checklist

☐ **Front-pouch baby carrier**

A pouch in which you "wear" your baby. Common brand: Snugli. Buy one in medium-weight cotton (not heavy corduroy, which limits the carrier to winter use), with broad, easy-to-adjust, padded shoulder straps, and a waist strap as well. Make sure you can put the carrier on and remove it without help.

☐ ***Winter bunting for front-pouch carrier**

The hooded, weatherproof Babysnug Super-Bunting fits over the carrier. It also doubles as a regular bunting for a winter newborn.

☐ ***Infant seat**

I've marked this "optional" because your baby can use his infant car seat indoors as a tiny lounge chair. A separate infant seat just for indoor use is a luxury. If you buy one, make it molded plastic. Lining can be vinyl, or easy-to-remove and washable fabric.

☐ ***Washable fabric liner for infant seat**

Necessary for a vinyl-lined infant seat.

☐ **High chair**

If you can, splurge on a high chair with wheels and a seat that adjusts for height. Otherwise, buy a standard high chair that feels very sturdy, has a big wraparound tray that you can attach and remove easily, and a padded vinyl seat.

☐ **Battery-operated swing**

The seat should recline as far as possible, so your infant can use it from about six weeks of age. Anything else is gravy. Some swings offer attachments that may suit your needs: a removable seat that doubles as an indoor infant seat, for example, or a detachable cradle that doubles as a small bassinet.

☐ **1 set of batteries for the swing**

☐ ***Walker**

Mobile and free, your baby will be ecstatic in a walker once he's able to sit up a little. Look for one that's adjustable for height and has a tip-resistant rounded base on casters. Walkers can be dangerous—the risks are discussed below.

☐ ***Intercom**

Good to have if you live in a large house, or might be out gardening while your baby naps. Unnecessary in an apartment or small house. Get a system you can travel with; an intercom built into a cute nursery lamp won't fit in your suitcase.

NOTES

What—No Playpen?

A lot of mothers can tell you that their playpens were a waste of money, and rarely used. Some pens get turned into oversized toy repositories, and some are useful only when visiting babies need a nap.

If you're an avid gardener and want your baby safe nearby, a playpen might be worth the money. Otherwise, you have many alternatives if you need to put the baby down for a while. Tuck him into his infant seat while you cook, and give him a running monologue on what you're doing. Plop him in the swing while you take a phone call (as long as you can see him, too). And if you're going to the bathroom, just carry him with you. Vacuuming? Wear him in the carrier.

You have little to worry about until he can roll over by himself (about 3 months), by which time your home should be childproofed.

A Swing May Be Your Best Investment

Swings are as hypnotic as pendulums and make a rhythmic noise as they go—a delicious combination for many babies. Perhaps they associate it with swaying near the mother's heartbeat while she walks. Whatever the reason, a swing is sometimes the only thing that can soothe a colicky baby. If it works for your baby, by all means sacrifice the floor space (about 3 feet by 4 feet) to this whirring appliance.

To keep a tiny infant from rolling around in the swing, use a head-hugging pillow that cradles his head in a little halo of padding.

You'll also see swings with cradle attachments so a newborn can lie flat—but whether you care to pay for something that outlives its usefulness in two months is a personal choice. I wouldn't do it, unless I wanted to use the attachment as a bassinet at night.

Swings come battery operated or windup, and parents have fierce opinions about which they prefer. My friend Lisa, mother of four, traded in her battery-operated swing for a windup model because she got tired of feeding it expensive D-cell batteries. When the windup swing wound down, her babies snapped awake, but they went back to their naps when she rewound it. I'd rather pay for the batteries and let sleeping babies lie, and that's what you'll find on my checklist. (Why can't they just make an electric swing?)

If you buy a windup swing, make sure it's the longest-running swing you can find. The record at the moment, which will probably be broken by other manufacturers, is forty-five minutes.

Finally, when swings are used as baby-sitters, the baby goes hungry for human contact. For this reason alone, some experts prefer the windup machine that keeps the parent coming back.

On secondhand windup swings, be sure the winding mechanism is completely enclosed. The exposed mechanisms on some old swings have burst, sending the shrapnel flying.

The Problems with Walkers

If you're a baby, a walker is heaven. You're snugly confined in its seat, yet free to explore and zoom around the house. Unfortunately, you're also free to fall down stairs, tip over at the edges of rugs, pull scalding electric kettles down by the cord, and sample poisonous houseplants.

On top of all that, a baby who relies too much on the walker for mobility—i.e., whose parents use the walker as a baby-sitter—may start walking later than usual, and have trouble un-learning the awkward gait that so neatly propelled the walker.

But a walker can be sheer pleasure if it's used on the ground floor of a house (no stairs) for short periods of time (perhaps thirty to sixty minutes a day) and under your very watchful eye.

A walker isn't for newborns. Wait until your baby can sit up somewhat and reach the floor with his feet before you put him in the seat.

Finally, don't buy an old walker at a garage sale. It may have exposed springs or hinges now prohibited by the Consumer Products Safety Commission.

Wearing Your Child

The carrier is a good habit to cultivate from birth, before your baby has time to reject it as some nuisance contraption.

A mother who wears her baby has more liberty than one pushing a carriage: it's easy to get a Snugli through a revolving door, and your hands are free for packages. Carriers create intimacy between parent and child, and the rhythm of your walking (or vacuuming) can be incredibly soothing. Some parents use these almost exclusively for housework.

There are two types of carriers for infants (as opposed to rigid-framed backpacks for toddlers): the *front pouch*, such as a Snugli, and the over-the-shoulder *cradle carrier*.

Your best bet is a front pouch made of medium-weight fabric. Avoid corduroy, even if it's winter—your body heat and the close embrace of the carrier can be sweltering. (Remember that babies overheat easily.) On the other hand, some mothers find that thin seersucker tears after a while. Denim and plain cotton are a good compromise. Advantages to the pouch: it offers lots of support; baby can't fall out; and Mom has both her hands free.

In cold weather, wear the pouch under your coat. You won't be able to button up, but at least you can remove your coat later on without disturbing your passenger. (A maternity coat will serve you nicely here.)

Try on several carriers in the store, if you can. These are the features of a good one:

- Wide, well-padded shoulder straps that adjust easily
- A broad waistband that keeps the pouch close to your body
- Easily washed
- Some head support for baby
- Soft or padded leg openings

• Snap-out bib to protect both carrier and mother's clothes from spit-up

• Strictly extras: inner flaps for discreet breast-feeding; detachable outer covering to add warmth in winter

If your baby rejects the front pouch after repeated trials (you'll know; he'll scream), exchange it for a cradle carrier. It's worn diagonally across the body with a single strap; the bag itself rests on your abdomen or your hip, and cradles the baby on his back. If you bend over, the bag falls away from your body, so you'll need a free hand to hold the bag close. Some babies are more comfortable in this natural position.

Again, look for a wide, well-padded shoulder strap that adjusts easily for length, and fabric that washes easily.

High Chairs, Plain and Fancy

Your baby won't need a high chair until he can sit up competently; until then, he'll eat in his infant seat or car seat when you start him on solid food. Still, many parents like to buy the high chair early.

A high chair on wheels, with a seat you can raise and lower, is more than worth the extra cost. You can wheel it out of sight when company comes, or onto the patio in spring. You can also lower it for easy feeding when the family's sprawled on the floor watching movies.

If you're economizing, buy a standard high chair. Most parents do, and the good chairs work out fine.

A good high chair, with or without wheels, will have these features:

• Broad, stable base that doesn't wobble
• Big wraparound tray that attaches and detaches easily
• Restraining straps, including crotch strap, that work easily

- A padded vinyl seat, for comfort and ease of cleaning
- Just enough space between the cushions so that you can dig out bits of food with your finger before they spoil

Don't buy a chair that tries to do everything, like one model that reassembles into a desk and seat. Security and simplicity are the key words here. You'll find a lot of good manufacturers, but for a standard mid-priced high chair, so many moms speak highly of Fisher-Price that it seems worth mentioning here.

Toys That Bounce

Babies love to bounce—but how much stuff can you have around the house? Here are two pieces of bouncing gear, both pleasurable but neither essential (and therefore not on the checklist).

Bouncer or bouncing seat. An inexpensive fabric hammock suspended in a heavy wire frame. When your baby kicks, the hammock bounces. This can keep him amused for a long time, and also props him up slightly for a nice view of the world. Put it on the family dinner table and let him coo while you converse.

Jumper. This seat hangs from a spring, which in turn hangs from the molding over your doorway, where it attaches with a big clamp. If your molding lies almost flat against the wall, it won't be safe. (You could buy a freestanding jumper, but that's a big sacrifice of space). Don't walk away for a second—when your baby pushes off from the floor and starts bouncing, he can bash his head into the door frame. The minimum age for a jumper is about four months.

A Note on Baby Gates

The old accordian-style baby gates are dangerous. As for new gates, they get pretty bad reviews. Consumer Reports, which tested them, found problems with every single gate—even the solitary model that it rated "satisfactory." Gates can kill, either by trapping a baby's head or neck, or simply by not standing up to a toddler's assault.

That's one reason you won't find gates on this checklist. The other is that you don't have to decide about gates until your baby is six or seven months old. If you do feel safer with gates blocking the staircase, buy those that mount with hardware, not simply with pressure, and check out the ratings in Consumer Reports' book *Guide to Baby Products*.

9
DIAPERS AND DIAPER SUPPLIES

A recent poll asked environmentalists what kind of diapers they used for their babies. About 80 percent confessed to using disposables. That says a lot about the seductive convenience of landfill-clogging plastic. My recommendation: buy two packages of disposable diapers and sign up for diaper service, too. If you don't like the cloth diapers, stop the service; you'll get a partial refund. And if you do stick with cloth, the disposables won't go to waste—you'll use them every time you take your baby outside.

You'll find two checklists here, one for disposables and one for cloth. *All* new parents need everything on the disposables list. The second list is for new parents who are trying a diaper service, too.

Checklist for Disposable Diapers

☐ **2 packages disposable diapers, size small**
Buy Pampers, Luvs, or Huggies: the big brands sometimes have more elastic around the leg openings. Diapers come 60 to a package; you'll use about 10 a day.

☐ **1 package diaper liners**

Liners absorb extra moisture. Use them inside disposable diapers at night so you won't have to change diapers with every feeding.

☐ **Diaper bag**

A good bag has three pockets (with waterproof lining) to hold bottles, a changing pad, and a broad shoulder strap. Buy one you really like; it will be your constant companion for about two years.

☐ ***1 dozen thick, prefolded cloth diapers**

Buy these *only* if you're not using a diaper service. They're for you, not the baby—tossed over your shoulder, a diaper will protect your clothes from a rivulet of spit-up and drool. Nothing else works as well.

☐ **1 diaper pail**

Order one from the diaper service if you're trying cloth diapers. Otherwise, buy a short plastic pail with a lock and a foot-pedal. (You'll need plastic garbage bags to fit.)

Checklist for Cloth Diapers

☐ **Diaper service**

Listed in the Yellow Pages. The service will typically deliver 80 diapers a week. Ask about refund policies before you pay.

☐ **2 water-resistant diaper covers, sized for newborns**

These thick cloth covers (also called wraps) slip on over the diaper, eliminate the need for diaper pins, keep the diaper from gushing through to clothes and bedding, and last through three or four diaper changes before they, too, get drenched and need laundering. Common brands: Nikkys, Biobottoms, Diaperaps. Your diaper service may sell them, too. If you stay with cloth diapers, you'll ultimately need 8.

☐ **2 pairs nylon or plastic pants, sized for newborns**

These completely waterproof pants (shaped like under-pants) are what your mother used for you. See how you like them compared with diaper covers—they're less convenient, requiring you to use pins or clips; but they're infinitely cheaper. Again, if you stay with cloth diapers, you'll ulti-mately need 8.

☐ **2 pairs of diaper clips**

Clips are much easier to use than pins—they work like tiny clamps, with no sharp ends to jab the baby, and no struggling to force them through several layers of cloth. Some diaper services sell them.

NOTES

Why Buy Brand-Name Disposables?

Until your baby starts eating solid foods, his waste will be nearly as liquid as his diet. You want a diaper that keeps leaks to a minimum. Brand-name disposables (Pampers, Huggies, Luvs) sometimes have twice as much elastic around the leg openings than generic, store-label, or biodegradable brands. Until leaks are no longer a problem and you can experiment with money-saving store brands, it's worth paying brand-name prices.

How Diaper Services Work

The service comes by once a week to pick up the dirty diapers and drop off a heavy-duty plastic bag full of clean ones. (Use that bag to line the diaper pail.) Typically, the service will try to sign you up for at least four weeks off the bat. If you cancel after a week or two, you'll typically get a partial or prorated refund.

Folding a cloth diaper for the first time will seem a little like origami. Try to get a friend to show you how.

Buying Covers for Cloth Diapers

A cloth diaper worn by itself would soak through in five minutes. Cloth covers and plastic pants are simply outer garments that prevent this. You can spend some serious money here, so experiment with different types of covers before you invest. Your options range from $1 plastic pants to $16 "breathable" wool covers—and not only will you need 8 pairs, but you'll need them in different sizes as your baby grows.

Whatever type of cover you choose is a matter of personal preference. These are your three main options:

Water-resistant covers. These thick cloth covers let some air reach the skin, which supposedly cuts down on diaper rash. Moisture will seep through, but not all at once. No diaper pins needed.

Waterproof covers. Also made of thick cotton or wool, these covers have an inner layer of plastic or nylon, and are designed to stay dry on the outside. (Some do, some don't.) No diaper pins needed.

Plastic or nylon pants. These are impermeable to moisture and very affordable—the big drawback being that you must use pins or clips to keep the diapers closed, and virtually no air circulates around your baby's bottom.

As long as you can reach for a disposable diaper, there's no rush to decide which diaper covers to buy. Take the time to find out which products will make cloth diapering easiest for you.

Cloth Diapers Aren't for Everyone

When Ari was a newborn, I could never pull the diapers tightly enough around his slender thighs to prevent leaks—and after two weeks of on-again, off-again trying, I switched to disposables for good. Two friends of mine with the same problem also switched to disposables—but then went back to cloth when their babies started eating solid food (about six months of age). That worked perfectly, because (a) their babies' thighs were no longer skinny, and (b) their babies' stool was not as runny.

A third friend never had the slightest trouble with cloth. Given those numbers, I do think cloth diapers are worth a shot.

What Goes in the Diaper Bag?

This is what parents cram into diaper bags, more or less:

1. Three disposable diapers
2. Three medium-size plastic bags, for disposing of soiled diapers
3. Diaper wipes (inch-thick stack) in sealed plastic sandwich bag
4. Facial tissues, small pack
5. Changing pad (for your baby to lie on during changes)
6. Cloth diaper for parent's shoulder
7. Extra bib, if baby is heavy drooler or spits up frequently
8. Extra pacifier, if baby likes them (one always falls to the ground)
9. Bottles, if baby is not breast-feeding
10. Sunscreen
11. Hat, if baby isn't wearing it

Try to make room for your wallet and comb, too, so you won't have to carry a purse.

10

TOYS

Your newborn has perfect vision for about six or eight inches—precisely the distance from your nourishing breast to your fascinating face. In fact, he's born with a fascination for faces. He also likes patterns and color combinations that offer strong contrasts—black-and-white stripes are a real hit.

Toys, for a newborn, are mostly a source of visual and tactile stimulation. Interesting textures, like towels and stuffed animals, show him—along with his mother's warm skin and flannel nightgowns—that the world is full of intriguing things to touch. Some toys teach cause and effect: when your infant is kicking exuberantly on the changing table, for example, place a squeak toy under his heels, or loosely tie a string from his ankle to the mobile overhead. (Don't turn away from him while the string is attached.)

A newborn can only handle so much visual stimulation at a time. In the first couple of weeks he may stare at you for just a few seconds at a time. So if he stares at a patterned picture for fifteen seconds and then starts crying, respect his wishes and take the picture away for now.

Avoid toys labeled for older age groups, because they may have tiny parts that could detach and choke a baby. (Sometimes that's all the age label means.)

Your baby only needs a handful of toys. These are some of the best:

Toy Checklist

☐ **Mobile**

A mobile should appeal to babies, who view it from below. One of the best (and least expensive) is the Stim-Mobile, which dangles faces and patterns in riveting black and white.

☐ **Play mat**

This is a small, bright quilt on which your infant lies facedown. He'll have plenty to explore, with his eyes or his fingers: colors, patterns, teething toys, mirrors, and fabrics of different textures. The whole thing can be tossed in the washing machine.

☐ **Rattle**

A newborn can't yet hold a rattle—but you can, and he may like to follow the sound and the motion. Rattles should be easy to grasp, far too big to swallow, nearly impossible to break. Any rattle that's part of gift wrapping should be thrown out; it's an ornament, not a toy, and almost certainly fails the federal safety standards.

☐ **Mirror**

An unbreakable mirror is a great toy. One version has black-and-white patterns on the back that are as fascinating to infants as the mirror's reflection. (Incidentally, he doesn't realize he's looking at himself.)

☐ **Squeak toy**

If it's easy to grasp and squeak, it teaches cause and effect. Your baby will enjoy looking at squeak toys with faces. Make sure the toy doesn't contain a squeaker that could detach and choke your baby.

☐ **Baby gym**

A baby gym is a toy-dangling apparatus that stands on four legs above your baby; he kicks the toys to set them

swinging. (Don't confuse this with a crib gym, which hang
over the crib, runs the risk of entangling an older baby'
clothes, and as a result should be removed at about fiv
months.)

☐ **Dolls and animals**

Anything with a clearly drawn face is interesting. Mov
it around and let him follow the toy with his eyes. (Don'
put stuffed animals in the crib; your newborn can't push
them away from his face.)

☐ **Magazine photos of faces**

Show your baby full-page photos of friendly, smiling
faces. He'll beam right back at them.

☐ **Teething toys**

At about three months and up, when your baby can grasp
things, he'll appreciate a good teething toy. One favorite is
a yellow, soft plastic sphere studded with short plastic "fingers." (Sold in The Right Start and other catalogs.)

NOTES

A Word about Crib Toys

The Consumer Products Safety Commission says that
dozens of babies have died when their clothes snagged on
crib toys, which include activity boxes, crib gyms, even
mobiles. The biggest problem with crib toys is that your
baby's alone with them while you're asleep, and he has no
concept of personal safety.

If you do follow tradition and hang a mobile over the crib,
remove it as soon as your baby can push up on his hands and
knees, or when he's five months old, whichever comes first.
Better yet, hang the mobile over the changing table instead.

How Can You Tell If a Toy Is Safe?

It shouldn't fit in a baby's mouth. The Consumer Products Safety Commission sets a minimum size, but it's too conservative. *New York Newsday* reported in 1990 that the plastic "Little People" figures by Fisher-Price meet federal standards, yet have choked babies to death.

How small is too small? According to federal safety standards, if a toy fits completely inside the plastic No-Choke Testing Tube, it's dangerous. (You can order the tube for $1 from Toys To Grow On, P.O. Box 17, Long Beach, CA 90801.) But use good judgment: marbles and paper clips pass this federal test; so do the "Little People" figures.

A TOUGHER TOY TEST

Here's a cheap, ultraconservative gauge for the safety of a small toy: Does it fit inside the cardboard tube from a roll of toilet paper? If it's too long *and* too wide to fit inside, it's probably safe.

It should be virtually indestructable. If it's plastic, can you break it or pull it apart? (You'll soon learn how to do this without being spotted by salespeople.) If it's a stuffed animal, can you dig out the glass eyes or pull off the button nose? Could a chewing baby split the seams and swallow the stuffing?

Snip off any bells, ribbons, cords, or strings, and peel off any stickers. Once your baby can use those little fingers, he may pull the stickers off by himself—and eat them.

11

LAUNDRY SUPPLIES

Babies don't just drool, spit up, and wet on their own clothes. They do it on yours. Formula stains are especially tenacious, and soiled clothes need fast attention. But there's one advantage to all this laundry: If you put a crying newborn in his infant seat on top of a rumbling washer or dryer, he may be soothed into blessed silence.

Laundry Checklist

☐ **1 box of baby-formulated detergent**

Common brand: Dreft. The baby-formulated detergent is less irritating to a newborn's skin than regular detergent.

☐ **Chlorine bleach**

For stains on light-colored fabrics. If the smell of bleach lingers, run clothing through the rinse cycle until it disappears.

☐ **1 stick of rub-on stain remover**

Typically, a liquid stain remover requires you to do the laundry immediately. But a rub-on stain remover (common brand: Stain Stick) lets you treat stains up to a week before you throw clothes in the wash.

☐ **Laundry hamper**

Line it with a plastic bag; a newborn's laundry is often soiled.

NOTES

Soap versus Detergent

Even a pure soap, like Ivory Snow, will destroy the flame resistance of your baby's sleepwear. Your other option, detergent, contains chemicals that may irritate a newborn's skin. That's why you need to start with a milder (and pricier) baby-formulated detergent.

If your baby appears to have no allergies after a month or so, try using your regular detergent. (Ask your pediatrician if you're in doubt about the allergies.) Toss a tiny shirt in with the family wash and let your baby wear it for an hour or two. If his skin shows no irritation, try it again the next day. Eventually you can throw all the family laundry in together, although some fastidious parents shudder at the thought.

For clothing other than flame-retardant sleepwear, soap is perfectly safe, and it works better than detergent if you have soft water (water with a low mineral content).

12

TRAVEL GEAR AND TRAVEL TIPS

Some babies are perfect travelers, slumping into sleep as you're backing out of the driveway. Others don't like the confinement of a car seat or the bustle of an airport and make their point strenuously. If you're driving or flying to visit grandparents, you may find that some of these travel products, many sold through catalogs such as The Right Start and One Step Ahead, can make the ride smoother. With the exception of glare screens, all of these items are optional luxuries—see what your needs are before you buy.

Travel Checklist

☐ **Glare screens**
   Essential for car owners, especially in summer. These are typically dark plastic sheets or perforated white ones that attach to the side windows and keep the sun out of your baby's eyes. They won't interfere with the driver's vision.

☐ ***Automobile organizer**
   A pocketed fabric organizer that hangs from the headrest.

☐ ***Rearview baby mirror**
   Attaches to the windshield with a suction cup; provides view of the backseat passenger.

☐ ***Cold pack**
For keeping bottles of milk cool.

☐ ***Portable bottle warmer**
A nylon bag that holds one bottle and contains a heat-releasing disc. Pinch the disc and the warmth spreads. To reuse, boil the bag.

☐ ***Zagat Restaurant Surveys**
Every Zagat restaurant guide has a listing in the back of restaurants that welcome young children. Zagat guides are published for thirteen U.S. cities and Montréal.

NOTES

Traveling with Your Baby

Newborns can make pretty good travel companions—they won't fight you for the window seat, and if you're lucky they'll sleep most of the way. But it's always a good idea to overpack the diaper bag—an extra outfit, extra sweater, extra pacifiers, extra diapers—so you can cope with any emergencies.

These suggestions may make plane or car trips a little easier:

When a plane takes off or descends for landing, your baby can clear his ears by sucking on a breast, bottle, or pacifier. Unless he's crying with hunger, try not to feed him in the thirty or sixty minutes prior to takeoff. (Remember that the plane can start rolling down the runway long before it gets permission to ascend.) Don't be upset if your baby cries during takeoff and landing; his ears may hurt, but the act of crying helps ease the pressure that's causing his discomfort.

• Use diaper inserts so you won't have to change diapers too frequently en route. A diaper insert (common brand:

Diaper Doubler) looks like a large sanitary napkin and increases the diaper's absorbency.

- Carry a couple of rattles and squeak toys for distraction.
- In a plane, don't be embarrassed by your baby's crying—every other parent in the plane will be sympathetic. If carts aren't clogging the aisle, put your baby against your shoulder and walk him up and down.
- Planes can be chilly and the seats are always cramped, so grab a blanket and a pillow as soon as you board. Tuck the pillow between your elbow and the armrest, or use it to prop up your baby's head for nursing.
- On a plane, try to reserve a bulkhead seat on the aisle. You can change the baby on the floor at your feet, and stand up to walk him if he cries.
- In a car, never take a crying baby out of his car seat for cuddling. An adult in the backseat can offer comfort and a bottle, however. One common cause of backseat crying is sun in a newborn's eyes; a Foreign Legion–style hat with its broad brim can be helpful here.
- To warm up a chilled bottle on a plane, ask the flight attendent for a pitcher half-filled with warm water and dunk the bottle inside. (Do this early in the flight, so the bottle is ready when your baby is. You might even run the bottle under warm water in an airport bathroom before you board.) For car trips, carry a Thermos of hot water, pour some into the Thermos cup, and stand the bottle in the cup.

Your newborn can spend an entire plane trip on your lap, but some parents feel safer if they pay for an extra seat and use their infant car seat on board. You can bring your car seat on board if it was made after January 1, 1981, and carries a sticker that says it meets "federal motor vehicle safety standards" or is "certified for use in motor vehicles and aircraft." Any car seat made today is airline approved; if you're in doubt about a secondhand car seat, call the manufacturer.

In cars and planes, never fasten your seat belt around both you and your infant. You can fatally crush him in a crash.

13

BEST MAIL-ORDER CATALOGS

Catalogs sell some terrific items that are hard to find in stores: hand-carved baby rattles, for example, or little heating pads to take the chill out of diaper wipes, or even plain cotton diapers, surprisingly hard to track down. Browsing through them while you're pregnant can be a pleasure. The list that follows, by no means exhaustive, is a sampling of the best.

☐ **After the Stork**
1501 12 St. NW
Albuquerque, NM 87104
505-243-9100
Cost: none
   All-cotton clothing in bright colors, sensibly priced.

☐ **Baby Björn**
c/o Sassy, Inc.
1534 College SE
Grand Rapids, MI 49507
616-243-0767
Cost: none
   Swedish diaper bags, baby carriers, travel bags.

☐ **Biobottoms**
P.O. Box 6009
Petaluma, CA 94953
707-778-7945
Cost: none
   Cloth diapers, many varieties of diaper covers, cotton
rompers, Foreign Legion–style sun hats.

☐ **Children's Wear Digest**
2515 E. 43 St.
P.O. Box 22728
Chattanooga, TN 37422
800-433-1895
Cost: $2
   Snowsuits, jumpsuits, and other brightly colored babies'
garments.

☐ **The Company Store**
500 Company Store Rd.
La Crosse, WI 54601
800-323-8000
Cost: none
   Flannel crib sheets, down-filled quilts, cotton sheets and
dust ruffles, cotton-filled bumpers. Also: down-filled mittens, booties, caps, buntings, and snowsuits for infants.

☐ **The Walt Disney Catalog**
1 Disney Drive
P.O. Box 29144
Shawnee Mission, KS 66201
800-237-5751
Cost: none
   Rompers adorned with Baby Mickey and Pluto; coveralls,
Disney mobile, Mickey Mouse dolls, bibs, crib linens.

☐ **Garnet Hill**
262 Main St.
Franconia, NH 03580
800-622-6216
Cost: none
   Expensive baby wear and crib linens made of natural fibers.

☐ **Hanna Andersson**
1010 NW Flanders St.
Portland, OR 97209
800-222-0544
Cost: none
   Possibly the best catalog anywhere for babies. Hanna Andersson sells soft cotton clothing, most of it made in Sweden. She also sells some maternity clothes and invites her customers to send back "hannadowns," or used clothes, in exchange for credit.

☐ **Hearth Song**
P.O. Box B
Sebastopol, CA 95473
800-325-2502
Cost: none
   Bright felt balls, goat-bristle baby brush, natural fiber stuffed bunnies.

☐ **Lands' End Kids**
1 Lands' End Lane
Dodgeville, WI 53595
800-356-4444
Cost: none
   Playsuits, snap-shoulder T-shirts, overalls, tiny sweat suits in bright colors and patterns..

☐ **Lillian Vernon**
510 S. Fulton Ave.
Mount Vernon, NY 10550
914-633-6300
Cost: none

Laundry bags, rattles, car organizers, crib linens, dishwasher cages for nipples and rings.

☐ **Maggie Moore**
170 Ludlow St.
Yonkers, NY 10705
914-968-0600
Cost: none

Buntings, blankets, diaper covers, hats, rompers, jumpsuits, and socks.

☐ **Mother Nurture—Everything for Breastfeeding**
916 Royal Blackheath Court
Naperville, IL 60563
708-420-4233
Cost: $3

Blouses, skirts, dresses, brassieres, and sewing patterns for breast-feeding mothers. "We can cross-check your measurements and the garments' measurements to give you a good fit." Returns are easy (they mark postage on the box).

☐ **Motherwear**
Box 114
Northampton, MA 01061
413-586-3488
Cost: none

Dresses, shirts, nightgowns, and brassieres for breast-feeding mothers; diaper knapsacks (instead of diaper bags), baby slings, and cotton diapers.

☐ Olsen's Mill Direct
1641 S. Main St.
P.O. Box 2266
Oshkosh, WI 54903
414-233-7799
Cost: $2
   Traditional OshKosh B'Gosh bib overalls in many colors.

☐ One Step Ahead
P.O. Box 46
Deerfield, IL 60015
800-274-8440
Cost: none
   Travel products, diaper bags, buntings, bottle warmers, linens.

☐ Patagonia
1609 W. Babcock St.
P.O. Box 8900
Bozeman, MT 59715
800-638-6464
Cost: none
   Cold-weather baby buntings, cardigans, and coveralls.

☐ The Right Start Catalog
Right Start Plaza
5334 Sterling Center Drive
Westlake Village, CA 91361
800-LITTLE-1
Cost: none
   Highly recommended for its large assortment of baby gear, including Foreign Legion–style sun hats, teethers, mobiles, diaper bags, and dishwasher cages for nipples and rings.

☐ Sears Infant & Toddler catalog
Order by telephone only:
800-366-3000
Cost: $1

A good source for cloth diapers.

☐ Sensational Beginnings
P.O. Box 2009
300 Detroit Ave., Suite E
Monroe, MI 48161
800-444-2147
Cost: none

Toys that shake, rattle, and roll; lullabies on cassette; and the amazing Skwish rattle in choice of black and white (for infants) or bright colors (for older babies).

☐ Seventh Generation
10 Farrell St.
South Burlington, VT 05403
800-456-1177
Cost: $2

Biodegradable diapers, cloth diapers, unbleached baby wipes, talc-free baby powder, and organic baby foods.

☐ Silk Oak
1343 Mecklenburg Rd.
Ithaca, NY 14850
607-277-0567
Cost: none

Rompers, T-shirts, and drawstring "baby bags," all silk-screened by hand with original designs of cows, bears, rabbits, and tigers.

☐ **The Wooden Soldier**
Kearsarge St.
North Conway, NH 03860
603-356-7041
Cost: none

Ravishing frills and frocks for girls and perfect-little-gentleman clothes for boys.

14

THINGS TO DO (AND WHEN TO DO THEM)

Getting ready for your baby isn't like planning a wedding: your baby will arrive whether you've made elaborate preparations or not. His only urgent needs are for love, food, and diapers—and you can send anyone out for diapers.

If you do have time, however, make as many preparations as you can before the birth—ideally by the end of the eighth month, in case you deliver early. (Most first-time mothers don't.) You can do these things in any order you like, although I've suggested a rough timetable here.

Checklist: Things to Do

Fifth or Sixth Month:

☐ **Sign up for Lamaze, Bradley, or other childbirth classes.**

Any class that prepares you for the birth will be invaluable. You'll understand more about what happens during labor and delivery, master some breathing techniques to help manage the pain of labor, turn childbirth into a team effort with the father (or a friend) as coach, and learn exactly what to expect in the hospital, from the admitting room to the maternity ward.

If the class does not include a tour of the maternity ward, arrange that separately. Also, because there's always the possibility of cesarean section, find out if fathers must see a film on C-sections before they can enter an operating room. (Don't panic—you'll see far more in the film than in surgery, where both parents' view is entirely blocked by a sheet.)

Seventh Month:
☐ **Order the crib and other furniture.**
If the store doesn't have it in stock, you may have to wait weeks for delivery.
☐ **Plug in to the borrowing network.**
Pregnant mothers can tap into a loosely linked but generous network of friends, friends of friends, and coworkers who will happily lend out their maternity and baby clothes, not to mention swings, high chairs, cribs, and toys.

Informal as it is, this network may amaze you—especially when a giant box of maternity and baby clothes arrives from a friend's friend in another state, with a note saying, "Please keep these or pass them on. I won't need them anymore." It's a favor you may return one day by lending things to someone else.
☐ **Start a "borrowed" list.**
Keep a running list, with brand names and careful descriptions of every item you borrow, of who owns what. ("Green shirt w/black stripe across chest and short sleeves, Carter label, size 6 mos.—borrowed from Barbara Brotman.") This list helps you remember who owns what, and it's nice to tell a mother who lends you things that you're keeping track.

(Conversely, if you ever lend someone your own maternity or baby clothes, include a list with your name, address, and description of each item. Keep a copy for yourself.)
☐ **Buy some good books about babies.**
Especially these four:

1. *Dr. Spock's Baby and Child Care,* by Benjamin Spock and Michael B. Rothenberg

2. *What to Expect the First Year,* by Arlene Eisenberg, Heidi E. Murkoff, and Sandee E. Hathaway

3. *79 Ways to Calm a Crying Baby,* by Diana S. Green

4. *The World of the Newborn,* by Daphne Maurer and Charles Maurer

And to restore your sense of humor in those first sleepless nights, I recommend *Surviving Your Baby & Child,* by Victor Langer.

☐ **Prepare your baby files.**

You'll need a safe, organized place to keep all that baby paperwork: medical records, birth certificate, social security card, hospital and doctors' bills, insurance paperwork, souvenirs (cards, letters, hospital I.D. bracelets), and the savings bonds that babies sometimes receive as gifts.

☐ **Update your home's fire safety.**

Not as much fun as shopping for baby clothes, but more important.

Install a smoke alarm on each floor, if you don't already have one.

Put new batteries in all smoke alarms. (Batteries should be replaced twice a year. It's easy to remember if you change them on Daylight Savings days, when you set your clock forward or back.)

Test the alarms.

Plan new escape routes that include the baby.

Purchase small fire extinguisher for kitchen, if desired. Read instructions.

Many fire departments will send you a home safety checklist if you ask.

☐ **Take care of car repairs.**

Anything that will make your car safer for its new passenger is worth doing in advance.

☐ **Start interviewing pediatricians.**

This is a long-term relationship, so you have to like the doctor, not just his or her credentials. You can get recommendations from friends, your obstetrician, or the hospital where you plan to give birth. Try to choose a pediatrician before you give birth.

What happens if you don't? The hospital will ask one of its own pediatricians to give your newborn his first checkup. You can keep seeing that doctor, or have your baby's medical records sent to the pediatrician you ultimately choose.

I urge you to read the first chapter of *What to Expect the First Year*—specifically, a ten-page section called "What It's Important to Know: Selecting the Right Physician."

Here are a few suggestions for your interviews:

Arranging the consultation: When you call, tell the receptionist that you are pregnant and want a consultation. A consultation, or initial interview, is sometimes free. Ask if there is a charge.

Bring a notebook, pen, and list of specific questions to the consultation.

Some key questions to consider: What is the doctor's position on breast-feeding? On circumcision? On mothers returning to work? On allowing an infant to cry?

How does the doctor handle emergencies . . . and non-emergencies? Does the doctor ever make house calls? Is the doctor board certified? How much does an office visit cost?

Is the doctor on call twenty-four hours a day? Who will see your baby when the doctor is on vacation? (It's a good idea to talk to that person, too.) What hospital is the doctor affiliated with?

And some criteria to consider: Do the doctor's attitudes support or conflict with your own? Are your questions treated with patience and respect? Are the doctor and the staff friendly and attentive? Can you afford the fees? Is the office clean, bright, and equipped with toys? Can you reach the office quickly and easily, especially in a rainstorm or rush hour?

Eighth Month:
☐ **Write a wish list.**

Virtually everyone you know will soon be chorusing: "So what do they *need?*"

That's why you write a wish list, naming all the things you want: receiving blankets, undershirts, crib sheets, car seat. Give copies to both grandmothers, a couple of key coworkers, the shower hostess, and one or two close friends. For a sample wish list, see the appendix.

Alternatively, you can register with department stores or large baby-supply stores, much as you would for a wedding.

☐ **Make a place for your baby to sleep.**

Many parents keep the newborn in their bedroom for several weeks or months. For a discussion of bassinets and other baby beds, see Furnishings, chapter 6.

☐ **Plan for someone to help you after the birth.**

Real help, not just company—someone to run out for diapers, assist with 2 A.M. feedings, take the baby when you need a nap, and teach you the skills of parenthood. Both parents need help; this is not solely for the mom.

Mothers and mothers-in-law can be terrific if you know they won't be critical or interfering. Or you might hire a sleep-in baby nurse for two or three days to teach you the basic skills; then, when she leaves, have a housekeeper come in two or three times a week, freeing you to care for the baby full-time. Whom you hire, and for how long, is purely a personal decision.

If money is no problem, however, try to have one to two weeks of help after a vaginal delivery, and two to three weeks of help after a C-section.

Housekeeper, baby nurse, or both? This may help you decide:

If you plan to breast-feed or want to care for the baby yourself, a housekeeper can free your time by taking over the cooking, shopping, errands, laundry, and cleaning. You can talk to domestic employment agencies, or ask friends and coworkers if they know any terrific housekeepers—or baby-sitters who do housework—who can give you a hand.

Before your due date, show the housekeeper around your house and neighborhood. That way, you won't have to escort her to the washing machine or supermarket the day you get home with the baby. Have everything ready for her when her new job starts, including a daily list of things that need doing and, if necessary, a hand-drawn map showing the supermarket, drugstore, and dry cleaners.

If you plan to bottle-feed or want serious help with baby care, consider a trained baby nurse. You can hire her for two days or two weeks; it's up to you. If she sleeps in, she can help with middle-of-the-night bottle feedings and let both parents rest. Talk to at least three agencies (listed under Nurses in the Yellow Pages). Here are some questions you might ask:

• What qualifications do the baby nurses have? Are they nurse's aides with home-care experience, certified personal-care aides, or certified home attendants? (All three are good qualifications.)

• How many references does the agency check? One New York agency, for example, checks ten references, gives each nurse a psychological test to make sure she's emotionally stable, and requires an annual physical checkup.

• Can the agency send you someone who will teach without taking over? This is crucial if you want the pleasure of giving the first bath or eliciting the first burp . . . and maybe all the other burps, too. Some baby nurses prefer a take-charge role. (Of course, you may want someone who can step in, take charge, and give you a badly needed rest.)

• What are the fees for a live-in nurse? For a daytime-only nurse? A part-time nurse? Will a live-in nurse expect her own room?

• Will the baby nurse help with grocery shopping, laundry, cooking? How is her job defined?

• If you'll be breast-feeding, will the agency send someone who can encourage you and help with any problems? Some baby nurses feel their role is diminished if you breast-feed; it certainly gives them less to do.

☐ **Design and prepare the birth announcements.**

Long before your baby arrives you can choose a printer, design the announcements, decide on the wording, buy the stamps, and prepare your mailing list. When you call from the hospital with your newborn's name and vital statistics, the printer can get started.

☐ **Make a stationery basket.**

Fill it with thank-you notes, blank notes, and at least one roll of stamps. Add a small notebook for recording gifts, the givers' names, and the date you acknowledged each present. (If you exchange it, note that, too.) Keep the basket by the bed, and seize some time between naps, walks, and feedings to get your thank-you cards out.

☐ **Make a cue card for the father.**

If he's going to be the birthing coach, write down the key breathing techniques he'll need to remember. (If you took Lamaze, your cue card will be covered with notes like "Ah-hee, ah-hee" and "Ah-hoo, ah-hoo." Save it as a souvenir.)

If the insurance company wants to be notified of the birth, write down the phone number.

☐ **Pack your hospital bag.**

Going into labor is no time to race around looking for your camera and clean socks.

Pack:

1. Anything your Lamaze, Bradley, or childbirth instructor suggested, such as a focal point or tennis ball
2. Your address book
3. Socks or slippers

4. Bathrobe
5. Nursing bra, 2 bra extenders, disposable nursing pads
6. Maternity outfit for mother to wear home
7. Outfit for baby to wear home, including hat and socks
8. Camera, fresh film
9. Makeup, personal toiletries
10. Clothes, pajamas, and toiletries for father, if he plans to spend the night (typically permitted in private rooms)
11. Snacks for father (to avoid numerous trips to cafeteria during labor)
12. List of items to be packed at the last minute, such as toothbrush, deodorant, snacks, etc.

☐ **Buy or borrow an infant car seat.**

By law, you can't drive the baby anywhere—even home from the hospital in a taxi—without a car seat.

☐ **Get the cameras ready.**

Buy new batteries and fresh film. Arrange to buy, borrow, or rent a video camera if you want movies of the homecoming. Videotapes of a newborn's first days are the kind of reruns you can watch forever.

If photographs are important to you, consider buying an auto-focus camera with telephoto lens. Babies' facial expressions are fleeting, and with an auto-focus camera you won't lose time fumbling with the settings. The telephoto lens lets you zoom right in on the baby's face, which gives the pictures a sense of intimacy.

☐ **Post emergency phone numbers on fridge or near phone:**

- Pediatrician, with address
- State poison control hotline (look in the front of the White Pages)
- Police
- Fire

- Pharmacy that delivers
- Pharmacy that's open 24 hours a day, with address
- Supermarket that delivers—and, ideally, lets you phone in a list and "shop" from your bed

After the birth, you may want to add:

- Understanding friend (note: she *must* be a mother herself) to call if you need advice or reach your wit's end. A classmate from Lamaze can often be helpful.
- Parents Anonymous (800-421-0353), a hotline for parents who feel overwhelmed by stress, anger toward a crying baby, or the sudden demands of parenting. (These are normal feelings; you'll experience them all at one point or another.)
- Maternity ward, if the hospital invites questions about baby care

☐ **Call insurance company for pre-authorization.**

Some insurance companies require you to tell them your due date in advance. They then authorize you to check in to the hospital, and give you an authorization number or code.

Call your hospital's maternity admissions department and give them both your due date and pre-authorization code. This saves you time and paperwork when you finally show up in labor.

☐ **Get a telephone credit card.**

You can't make long-distance phone calls from a hospital room, unless they're collect or charged to your home phone.

☐ **Take a baby first-aid and CPR class.**

Call the American Red Cross in your area for information. The hospital where you plan to deliver may also have information on these classes. If you can't find one, buy or rent a videotape on the subject.

Ninth Month and Beyond:
☐ **If you'll need a full-time sitter, start spreading the word.**

If you have a job to return to, ask friends, coworkers, and neighbors if they know of any terrific sitters who will need work at about the same time. You may not be able to line your sitter up months in advance, but you want all these people to think of you when they hear of someone good.

Appendix
WISH LIST

When relatives, friends, and coworkers start planning your baby shower or asking what you need, it helps to give several key people—including the shower hostess, and both sets of the new baby's grandparents—a copy of your wish list. What follows is a sample wish list to edit and use as you please. Most of the items are moderately priced; all are satisfying to give. You'll also find a few products not in the book, simply because they're gifts you might enjoy.

As for the few big-ticket items, you'll be happier with the results if you shop first, decide what you want, and make a note of the brand and model that you prefer.

That brings us to the special role of the people who hold this list. They can help you best by keeping the list private—and making suggestions, when asked, without mentioning how many of each item you need. Gift givers will enjoy hearing at least four suggestions; it gives them the pleasure of choosing the present, not simply buying what you request.

Finally, the numbers on this list are for the list holder's reference. She'll know not to send a dozen relatives after the one diaper bag you need, and if she can learn what gifts people are buying, she can cross those items off her list.

Note your color preferences and any other wishes at the end, but make them easy to work with. (My wish list said, "We love pure white, sophisticated black, and all primary colors." It also noted that we were crazy about everything in the Hanna Andersson clothing catalog, and provided the toll-free number.) The trick is to steer people gently in the direction you want, without handing them a marketing list.

WISH LIST

Summer baby:

- [ ] 6 snap-crotch, short-sleeved undershirts, size 6 months
- [ ] 4 drawstring nightgowns, one size only
- [ ] 2 cotton sun bonnets with brim, sized for newborn
- [ ] 2 one-piece summer outfits with snap-crotch, size 6 months

Winter baby:

- [ ] 4 long-sleeved undershirts with side snaps, size 6 months
- [ ] 4 sleepers or stretch suits, size 6 months
- [ ] 4 long-sleeved jumpsuits or coveralls, size 6 months
- [ ] 2 drawstring nightgowns, one size only
- [ ] 2 zip-front nightgowns (also called blanket sleepers), one size only
- [ ] 2 warm hats
- [ ] 2 warm blankets
- [ ] Snowsuit with feet (September baby—size 12 months; December baby—size 6 months) or bunting (for babies born in February or March)

All babies:

- ☐ Diaper bag
- ☐ 6 terry-cloth bibs—the bigger the better
- ☐ 3 receiving blankets
- ☐ 2 hooded towels and 4 mitt-style washcloths
- ☐ 3 crib sheets, cotton knit
- ☐ Set of fabric bumpers for crib
- ☐ Play mat
- ☐ Unbreakable mirror
- ☐ Mobile (recommended: Stim-Mobile)
- ☐ Front-pouch baby carrier (brand _____, model _____)
- ☐ Infant car seat (brand _____, model _____)
- ☐ Intercom
- ☐ Swing (brand _____, model _____)
- ☐ Photograph albums
- ☐ Picture frames
- ☐ Unbreakable baby dishes
- ☐ Magazine subscriptions *(Parents, Parenting, Child, Working Mother)*

Our favorite colors for baby clothes: _____
Our favorite store or catalog: _____

About the Author

Dylan Landis is a former newspaper reporter who covered medicine for *The* (New Orleans) *Times-Picayune* and design for the *Chicago Tribune*. Her articles on business, health, and decorating have run in *The New York Times, House Beautiful, Metropolitan Home,* and other publications. The mother of one son, she lives in New York City.